Praise for *Delivering the Goods*

The supply chain is corporate America's last frontier. Conquering it is the key to reducing costs and maximizing profits. Damon Schechter and Gordon Sander have done a remarkable job of demonstrating the importance of supply chain management to today's business. They also show how the art of supply chain management evolved out of the military art of logistics, and how the most successful military leaders, from Alexander the Great on, were, for the most part, successful supply chain managers as well. Great reading and a must for any forward-looking business executive's library.

> —William "Gus" Pagonis, Senior Vice President
> of Supply Chain, Sears, Roebuck and Co.;
> Lieutenant General, U.S. Army (retired)

Delivering the Goods is an important milestone in helping educate business executives in the importance of logistics. Schechter and Sander skillfully articulate both the historic and contemporary value of logistics, making the book a must-read for any executive looking to enhance customer satisfaction and reduce the cost of doing business.

> —Yossi Sheffi, Director, MIT Center for
> Transportation Studies

With *Delivering the Goods*, Schechter and Sander have taken a previously neglected aspect of business and shown how supply chain management can transform an enterprise. Using examples from military history and modern industry, they show conclusively that sound logistics and their Tri-Level View can improve any organization's bottom line.

> —David Kelley, CEO, IDEO Product Development,
> the creators of the Apple mouse

Logistics is the basis of strategy in the business world, as well as the military. In *Delivering the Goods*, the authors accord it the importance it deserves.

> —Sir John Keegan, best-selling author of *The Face
> of Battle* and *A History of Warfare*

A fascinating history of logistics coupled with a pragmatic approach for turning your supply chain into a strategic differentiator. This is a great book to get marketers and supply chain leaders on the same page!
—Ralph Drayer, former Chief Logistics Officer,
Procter & Gamble

Damon Schechter and Gordon Sander have made a valuable contribution to management thought. Their book, *Delivering the Goods*, is exceptionally clear. Readers who had the benefit of learning logistics during their military service will appreciate the attention that this book provides. Other readers will benefit from their application of the Tri-Level View, which the authors use to extend business logistics into supply chain management. The Tri-Level View is an interesting concept, one that is fresh.
—Robert Delaney, author of the annual
State of Logistics Report

The book is terrific and fun to read. Damon Schechter and Gordon Sander discuss past business logistical practices of firms like Ford and Sears, and ask why so many firms today have not followed in their footsteps, given current market realities. The book is bound to enlighten all those looking for a better understanding of what it takes to compete and survive in today's marketplace.
—Robert Tamilia, Professor of Marketing,
University of Quebec at Montreal

Delivering the Goods is reminiscent of my entire 30-year career in logistics, from the military's longtime mastery of the field to the business world's recent recognition of its strategic importance. This is the first book I have read which contains an insider's perspective of both the military and business facets of this exciting field. It is an excellent primer for what is likely to be the most important field of business management during the coming decade.
—John Kenny, Vice President of Logistics, 3Com Corp.

Supply chain management has become the key differentiator for today's competitive business world, and *Delivering the Goods* is one of the best books that I have read for conceptualizing this often misunderstood field. Schechter and Sander have refreshing viewpoints, drawing a particularly great analogy between military and business logistics.
—Hokey Min, Executive Director, Logistics and
Distribution Institute, University of Louisville

Effective, integrated supply chain management can and does generate enormous value for organizations, particularly those with global distribution needs. The authors creatively compare modern business cases with military-based logistics scenarios to demonstrate the need for supply chain efficiency and the importance of logistics for today's managers.

—John Allan, Chief Executive, Exel

Damon Schechter and Gordon Sander have clearly illustrated the importance of logistics and supply chain management to business success. The historical context demonstrates how logistics and supply chain skills are both critical today just as they were in the past. In addition, the Tri-Level View provides managers a framework for better management.

—Donald Rosenfield, Director, MIT Leaders for
Manufacturing Fellows program; author of *Modern
Logistics Management*

Damon Schechter and Gordon Sander get it . . . business is war! Companies like Wal-Mart, Procter & Gamble, and Toyota have created tremendous shareholder value by embracing supply chain management as a competitive weapon. In *Delivering the Goods*, the authors skillfully convey the elevation of logistics as a key differentiator on the battlefields of business based on the lessons of successful military campaigns.

—John Lanigan, CEO, Logistics.com; Commanding
Officer of a Coast Guard Port Security Unit during
Operation Desert Storm

Damon Schechter and Gordon Sander bring a fresh approach to business logistics. Their tri-level model and analogies to military logistics ensure their book is far more insightful and interesting than a typical how-to tract.

—Graham Sharman, Professor of Logistics and
Supply Chain Management, Technical University of
Eindhoven, The Netherlands

Both as a consultant and as a venture investor I have seen the critical importance of supply chain management in creating competitive advantage for the few who master it, as well as the disadvantage for the many who do not. *Delivering the Goods* is all about obtaining that advantage.

—Geoffrey Moore, best-selling author of *Crossing the
Chasm*

Damon Schechter and Gordon Sander have delivered a very readable and entertaining book that examines the importance of logistics in supply chain management. The examples are lively and comprehensive, and the authors' tracing of the development of logistics in the business enterprise is a fascinating and informative narration that "makes history come alive." Overall, *Delivering the Goods* is a recommended read for those involved in the day-to-day practice of supply chain management.

—James Stock, Professor of Marketing,
University of South Florida; coauthor of
Strategic Logistics Management

Damon Schechter and Gordon Sander take the reader on a far ranging historical ride, highlighting the importance of logistics to military victory through the ages. What is the relevance of this to modern business? Critical, the authors argue, and provide insights and tools aimed at improving the performance of both public and private enterprises today.

—Sheila Widnall, Professor of Aeronautics and
Astronautics, MIT; Secretary of the
U.S. Air Force, 1993–1997

Delivering the Goods uses historical perspectives and concise case examples to bring a much needed clarity to the definition of logistics, while also presenting a compelling case for the value that can be gained by managers who improve logistics as a top business priority. The core tenets of this book represent the same values and business-results orientation that are key drivers of Ryder's worldwide logistics and transportation solutions.

—Gregory Swienton, CEO, Ryder System, Inc.

DELIVERING THE GOODS

The Art of Managing Your Supply Chain

DAMON SCHECHTER
with GORDON SANDER

JOHN WILEY & SONS, INC.

Published by John Wiley & Sons, Inc., Hoboken, New Jersey.

Published simultaneously in Canada.

For general information on our other products and services please contact our Customer Care Department within the United States at (800) 762-2974, outside the United States at (317) 572-3993 or fax (317) 572-4002.

Wiley also publishes its books in a variety of electronic formats. Some content that appears in print may not be available in electronic books.

Library of Congress Cataloging-in-Publication Data:

Schechter, Damon.
    Delivering the goods : the art of managing your supply chain / Damon Schechter, Gordon Sander.
       p. cm.
    Includes bibliographical references and index.
    ISBN 0-471-21114-1 (cloth : alk. paper)
    1. Business logistics. I. Sander, Gordon F. II. Title.
HD38.5 .S34 2002
658.7—dc21   2002069198

Printed in the United States of America.

10 9 8 7 6 5 4 3 2 1

To my parents, who have been caring
teachers, honest critics, great friends.
For so many reasons, without them
this book would not exist.
—D.S.

Contents

Preface

"The more and more I observe of modern war," British Field Marshal Harold Alexander wrote in his memoirs of World War II, in which he saw action and supervised Allied operations in numerous theaters of that far-flung war, "the more and more convinced I am that success in war depends on mastering that field which Americans call logistics."

Similarly, the more I have studied business, both as a student of and consultant to the corporate world, the more convinced I am that how efficiently and effectively a company manages its logistics is the key to victory on the contemporary business battlefield.

I was not the first person to make this deduction. Business experts of various stripes have been trying to get people to pay more attention to logistics—or distribution, as this recondite field was designated in the 1950s and 1960s, or supply chain management, as it is now called—for decades.

Even though transportation and distribution costs comprise one-fifth or more of sales for a typical American company, it was not clear that many people outside of a few traditionally logistically far-sighted companies like Sears Roebuck, and Wal-Mart understood this.

Only recently, in the wake of the burst of the dot.com bubble has the importance of successful logistics come to be widely accepted. The end of the dot.com bubble (like its eighteenth century predecessor, the South Sea Bubble) can be attributed in large part to the neglect of the supply side of business, as well as to the short-sightedness of the sales-based marketing philosophy that governed American business for most of the post–World War II period.

At most American companies, until as recently as five years ago, the supply side of business was still the *far* side of business. Few future leaders aspired to the supply side. However, today logistics—and logisticians—have, deservedly, moved to the center of the corporate stage. More and more, America's business leaders have returned to that sound early twentieth-century equation, which held that *creating* demand was only the first half of the marketplace challenge and that *satisfying* demand—including and especially satisfying the end customer's natural demand for speedy and accurate delivery—was the other requisite half.

Despite this belated coming of consciousness, as I made my way through America's logistical jungle, and came up with an easy-to-understand-and-apply formula for schematizing any company's logistics in the process—the Tri-Level View—I continued to be struck by the absence of a readable guide to this undeservedly neglected subject. This book is dedicated to rectifying that deficiency.

One of the reasons it has taken so long for logistics to be appreciated, especially in an image-conscious culture like America's, is the widely held perception that logistics is boring.

The first half of this book illuminates the origins of logistics as a military art, and presents, in effect, the story of war from the supply side. It includes an analysis of many of the great captains of logistics, beginning with history's arguably greatest logistician, Alexander the Great, the scourge of the Near East. Then we move on to Norman Schwarzkopf, the hero of the Gulf War, and his equally heroic logistician, Gus Pagonis. Then we segue into the more recent and intrinsically related evolution of business logistics. As you will see, logistics—or supply chain management—is important to success on *both* the military and corporate battlefields. In fact, it is essential. Most of the qualities that define the great captains of history—especially their foresightedness, flexibility, and resourcefulness—also are the qualities that define the successful, logisitically astute corporate leader.

The second half of the book is the how-to part that describes the Tri-Level View, my easy-to-use formula for schematizing and rationalizing your company's logistics, using various case studies from my back pages.

Enjoy. Use it up. Make it do.

—Damon Schechter

DELIVERING THE GOODS

Prologue

This book is divided into two related but discrete parts. The first half, *Supply and Command, A Journey through Time*, is the story of a traditionally neglected and poorly understood field: logistics.

After we explore some of the most inventive solutions ever devised for military and business logistical problems in the first half, the second half of this book, *Cracking the Code and Applying the Code*, applies the lessons learned to modern business. The lessons are incorporated into a formula that I call the Tri-Level View. The Tri-Level View is my easy-to-use formula for looking beyond the physical and political boundaries that are currently constraining and restraining you, whether you realize it or not, and breaking down the walls separating you and the other members of your supply chain. My hope, quite simply, is that this formula helps you deliver goods to your customers faster, easier, and less expensively.

If you're a current or future manager who picked up this book hoping for a brief account of how to improve your logistics system, you should skip ahead to the second half, *Cracking the Code and Applying the Code*. Otherwise you will benefit from the historical context provided by the first half.

For you officers and officer cadets out there, you will be most interested in the history of military logistics detailed in the first half, as well as the second half's details of how to deal with the problems and challenges of moving goods from the factory to the supply depot to the troops.

You marketers will be most interested in the first half's history of business logistics, particularly how marketing has become overly concerned with *creating* demand, instead of taking equal responsibility for managing the supply chain—*satisfying* demand—the other (often overlooked) half of marketing.

Investors will appreciate the first half's contention that amateur CEOs speak of tactics whereas professional CEOs speak of logistics, and the second half's easy-to-understand-and-apply formula for evaluating any company's logistical savvy.

History buffs will most appreciate the comprehensive while easy-to-read history of military and business logistics in the first half, including profiles of such diverse and pivotal figures—albeit sometimes involuntarily so—in military and business logistical history as the military commanders and generals Alexander the Great, Hannibal, Napoleon, the Duke of Wellington, Henry Kaiser, Gus Pagonis, and Norman Schwarzkopf; and business leaders, consultants, and educators Archibald Shaw, Henry Ford, Sam Walton, Philip Kotler, Keith Oliver, as well as others, in addition to illuminating the logistical aspect of such famous business failures as the South Sea Bubble and the recent dot.com bubble.

■ THE TRI-LEVEL VIEW

Where does it come from? Why is it important? And how will it help you analyze and solve your company or organization's problems? These are some of the questions answered in this section, a walk down the road that would ultimately lead me to develop the Tri-Level View.

■■■■■

My first step on this road began back in 1990, as a student of David Kelley, the famed founder of IDEO. Founded in 1978 in the heart of what would soon become known as Silicon Valley,

IDEO is America's largest independent product design and development firm, while Kelley enjoys a reputation as the "most sought after designer in the Western world," as *Fortune* once called him. He also has been called his generation's Thomas Edison. Employing both his knack for visual thinking, and linking that thinking to bona fide and real world customer needs, Kelley's wide-ranging innovations and products have included the Apple mouse, the Palm handheld computer, Polaroid's I-Zone instant camera, and an electric vehicle charging station, amongst many, many others.

In addition to his position at IDEO, David Kelley is also a professor in the Stanford University Product Design Program. As at IDEO, Kelley has successfully created in his classes at Stanford that rarest of things in the design and manufacturing world, or, for that matter, anywhere in the business world: a culture of true creativity, a place where both he and his students (of whom I was privileged to be one) can come up with truly useful things by "visualizing possible futures," as Kelley puts it.

Each year, on the first day of his popular class, Human Values in Design, Kelley strides into the room carrying two bulging suitcases. For two hours, like a mad door-to-door salesman, he then proceeds to pull out one apparently handy gadget or contraption after another.

The only problem is, as Kelley effectively demonstrates to his laughing students, that none of these products really are actually handy. In fact, most of them don't even work. A few—like a sexy, straight-from-the-factory can opener that, he shows, is guaranteed to slice your thumb off—are downright dangerous. It doesn't take long to get Kelley's point—that in their arrogance or stupidity, the designer and manufacturers of these absurd and even dangerous products have brought them to the market without properly testing them for either their safety *or* their desirability.

Thus, Kelley effectively demonstrates that if the age-old truth about necessity being the mother of invention—particularly worthwhile *and* profitable inventions—is still ever true, so is its obverse: that the absence of necessity, or customer need, can lead to some real lemons. Kelley's corollary, you might call it.

Recently the efficacy of Kelley's corollary was dramatically driven home in the larger, real world just beyond Stanford's walls, amidst the hi-tech hills and dales of nearby Silicon Valley, when dozens of Internet start-up companies, including numerous once highly touted ones, went belly up. Why? Because, in the vast majority of cases, these misguided companies had plunged into designing, building, and implementing their sexy, cool, computer-based services while presuming that Joe Q. Public was interested in these services in the first place—or even, in some particularly obtuse cases, without even seeing whether the technology for delivering them to Joe and his family actually worked.

A recent and quite spectacular proof of Kelley's rule—you could call it the look-before-you-leap-into-the-market rule—was provided by the catastrophic burnout of boo.com, the much-ballyhooed, London-based Net shopping service that reportedly went through more than $120 million before flaming out. When they started out in 1998, the young Swedish founders of boo.com, Kajsa Leander and Ernst Malmsten, had ambitions of being the upscale, readymade cyber-clothier to the world. Flush with start-up capital and cocksure of themselves, the two high-flying founders speedily hired a worldwide staff of about three hundred and established satellite offices around the United States and Europe. Photos of the ultraglamorous cyber-entrepreneurs appeared in magazines and newspapers around the world.

Alas, both Leander and Malmsten were so certain of themselves that they had not bothered to ascertain whether the average high-street shopper really *wanted* to buy his or her clothing off the Net—some did, most didn't—or even whether boo.com's much-vaunted, multifaceted, but, ultimately, hopelessly clumsy cyber-rack even worked.

It did not, and neither did boo.com. In May, 2000, less than two years after its bubbly take off, boo.com and its high living founders returned to Planet Earth—with a devastating thud, as the entire staff was fired *en masse* and the founders beat a hasty retreat.

Why? In Kelley-esque terms, Leander and Malmsten had, for all practical purposes devised a big can opener that didn't work.

Common sense? Perhaps. But many—far too many—supposedly cutting-edge manufacturing and services companies lack fundamental common sense in the way they design, plan, market, *and* manufacture things. And, far too many overlook perhaps the most important aspect of their product or service: ensuring that it can be delivered accurately, on-time, and in the right quantity.

Perhaps Leander and Malmsten should have taken a class with David Kelley. If so, they would have learned that to be a designer—a successful designer—it is imperative to think and act like a person, a *real* person. They might have paid more attention to the unglamorous but very real need and desire on the part of their potential customers for their product to be delivered accurately, on time, and in the right quantity, something that they obviously ignored, as did many other of their fellow failed dot-commers. The lesson that Kelley inculcates in his students is that no matter how brilliant you think your product or design is, it's best to consider it from every possible human perspective—including the delivery perspective—*before* going public with it.

The materials for Kelley's humanistic design courses include a number of valuable texts. Perhaps the most interesting of these is a primer on problem-solving called *The Universal Traveler*. Seeking to delineate the common denominators in all creative problem solving, Don Koberg and Jim Bagnall—themselves university design instructors at California Polytechnic State—interviewed and observed problem solvers from diverse walks of life, including everyone from philosophers to generals. There may even have been a logistician in there (historically, as you will see in the next section, a good many of the great supply chain innovators have, in fact, *been* generals), although I tend to doubt it.

But Koberg and Bagnall certainly talked to a good mix. Amongst other things, the two authors discovered that all of their exemplary problem solvers shared two traits, "an overweening curiosity about things" and "a drive to make things 'tick' better"—two of the traits that Kelley fused together and nurtured in me. This also happened to be the first prerequisite for me attaining the Tri-Level View.

Unfortunately, however, the program ignored what I saw as the concomitant need for future designers to build up their equally vital *business* sense. That is, to cater to, and develop both my left, designing side, and my right, business side—to be both a successful designer *and* a successful businessperson. And so, with Kelley's encouragement and blessing, I devised a curriculum for myself with courses from Stanford's Graduate School of Business, in addition to the ones I was taking at the engineering school, that would meet this pressing need *for me*.

■ ■ ■ ■ ■

Perhaps the most influential part of my business training was learning the following system of presenting and framing solutions to business problems: (1) Diagnosis: Cut through the fog to the critical issue and/or problem; (2) Decision: Succinctly state the solution to the problem; (3) Analysis: Expand upon the who, what, when, where, why, and how of the solution, for example, economic analysis, ethical analysis, and so on; (4) Reality Test: Talk about contingency plans—what should be done in case things go wrong, as they are bound to do. As you will see, this system can be used to analyze and solve *your* company's problems.

These are some of the questions you ought to be asking yourself as you prepare a diagnosis: Why is your company's share of the market shrinking? Why are profit margins getting smaller? Why do you have such large fluctuations in inventory?

As you know, the world is a very volatile place. Are you truly prepared for globalization and the move toward a world economy? Today's world economy is an increasingly interdependant one. Consequently companies of all shapes and sizes are looking abroad for new ways with which to expand their businesses, both by finding new customers to buy their goods, as well as new trading partners to help them build their goods.

As you are reading this, your competitors are busy allying with their trading partners in order to be more resourceful and aggressive at going after *your* customers. What is your response to this? At first blush, your answer might be to simply emulate the competition and unify with *your* own trading partners. However once long-term contracts are in place, and blood is exchanged (so to speak), it is difficult to say, "I'm going to cut costs 10 percent this year." Cutting costs can no longer mean simply flipping these costs over to a trading partner. You need to cut them yourself.

More questions: Are you prepared for increasingly volatile demand for your product or service (i.e., consumers deciding they can't get enough computer equipment one day, and then deciding they have more than enough equipment for the next)? Information, including news, now moves around the world at the speed of light, and the ability to instantaneously react to this information is par for the course. This means an emphasis on flexibility. Companies which can quickly adapt to fluctuations in demand, and get access to the information that helps them do so, will be best able to balance order sizes, frequency of orders, production schedules and delivery windows regardless of what comes over the newswire.

Consider, too, are you plagued by your industry's volatility, as your entire industry struggles with globalization, competition, and demand volatility, and the other members of your industry go through phases of rapid growth and contraction? Industry cycles are also par for the course. Be prepared for them. Sounds like common sense, but a surprising number of managers are not.

Also, are you trying to do things beyond your core competence? Many organizations are just beginning to focus on their strengths, and find partners to mitigate and overcome their weaknesses.

Ask yourself: Is your company's product or service following the general trend, morphing into a commodity? Commoditization is an increasing fact of life. Customers are finding that diapers are interchangeable whether they come from Wal-Mart or Kmart, ditto that computers are the same whether they are made by Dell or Hewlett-Packard. Increasingly, the factor that customers use to distinguish the various increasingly interchangeable brands for themselves is delivery, such as which diaper maker or computer manufacturer *can deliver the goods* to them in the proper quantity and assortment, as well as who can offer them at the cheaper price.

Is your product's increasing complexity cause for concern? Whereas only a few dozen parts went into Henry Ford's Model T at the time of its introduction all the way back in 1908, today thousands of parts go into making an automobile. Cooperating and sharing information with all the parties responsible for all these parts is increasingly important—and difficult.

After making your corporate diagnosis using the above parameters, you are ready to proceed to crack your company's supply chain code. At a loss for any Stanford-taught structure or framework to use here, I found myself a second step closer to attaining the Tri-Level View. As you will see, in the section *Cracking the Code and Applying the Code*, the Tri-Level View fills this void, helping you conduct a comprehensive analysis as well as make a pragmatic and innovative decision based upon it.

Finally, you need to identify the key risks of moving ahead with your action plan. These are some questions for your contingency planning, your reality test: What do you do in the event of budget problems or scheduling problems? What do you do in case of an earthquake or attack by terrorists? Unfortunately, as we saw on September 11, 2001, they are a part of reality, too.

Ask yourself, too: How intelligent are your policies and procedures you have in place in the event of a sudden breakdown in your supply chain? Having all the members of a team hop on a plane to meet face-to-face is nice from a theoretical point of view, but not very realistic. With less and less face time, organizations need to cooperate and adapt their policies and procedures to this new virtual, less personal world.

Gus Pagonis, the genius of the Gulf War, who crossed the military/civilian divide and now runs the logistics of Sears, Roebuck, and who is one of the role models for this book, is a strong believer in teleconferencing—with a caveat. He warns that "if you had an inefficient meeting before, it's really going to be disastrous if you try to do it telecommunicating. So I think that the whole business world is in for a huge wakeup call." Translation: Better technology doesn't necessarily make for a better meeting. First, the minds who go into that meeting have to give some considered thought to what they want to accomplish in that meeting, or else the result will simply be televised bedlam. Mixed-up minds will make for a mixed-up meeting, whether it is televised or not. This means that all of the members of your logistical team have to know your company's logistics, including your fallback system in case of a September 11 or similar disruption *before* the emergency takes place.

What *are* your contingency plans in the event of an all out disaster? On the morning of September 11, after the first plane had hit the World Trade Center, and even before the second plane hit 18 minutes later, General Pagonis quickly activated his contingency operations center at Sears. Consequently, Pagonis knew and was able to tell his CEO and commanding officer where all of the company's trucks were at that point in time, which ones were stranded, which couldn't get through customs, where his containers were, which stores were closed, what malls were closed, what tunnels were closed, and so on and so forth. Having practiced for such a contingency on numerous occasions, as well as having the operations to deal with it in place, Pagonis and his corporate logistics team were ready to switch into lock-down mode at a moment's notice. Consequently, there was no breakdown in the Sears supply chain at all. Although Pagonis's team had to go to 24/7 mode, as did similar logistics teams at corporations around the country, Sears suffered virtually no logistical problems at all. Even with FedEx grounded for three days, Pagonis and his team were still able to deliver the goods.

How well did *your* company respond to September 11? How good are *your* contingency plans? Are you as prepared as Sears was for a sudden disruption to *your* supply chain?

■ ■ ■ ■ ■

My next steps on the road to the Tri-Level View came inch by inch, as a consultant to the corporate world, as I got my mind's eye around the knotty problem of the grossly *inefficient* delivery systems by which many, if not most, companies use to ship their beer bottles and sundry other goods to their hapless, unseen customers.

To get a coherent idea of what a factory delivery and distribution system actually *was*, I spoke to a wide range of supply chain managers at logistically challenged, delivery-impaired, firms around the country.

To be sure, there already existed a growing body of reliable and usable knowledge about supply chain management. Amongst the knowledge leaders in this field are Stanford's renowned Hau Lee, and consultants like Booz Allen & Hamilton's equally renowned Keith Oliver, as well as successful practitioners like Pagonis and others. Unfortunately, however, I found their knowledge was not getting out there, into the corporate trenches, where it was most needed—at least not as much as it should have. American business as a whole remained surprisingly uninformed about the principles of logistics and supply chain management. I personally met many supply chain managers—or whatever their widely varying and often comical titles were—who had not the faintest idea of what they were doing. To them a delivery system was a dark inchoate thing.

And then one day, after wandering through the logistical wasteland, it came to me:

The Black Box.

Every delivery system, it struck me, is a black—or opaque—box. Goods are dropped into one end of this hypothetical box; at the other end, they are delivered. But, in between, what? *Something* happens. But *what*, exactly? Few of the supply chain managers really knew what happened inside their respective boxes. All they knew, essentially, is what they put into their boxes and what came out, that is, what was delivered to their customers. In between lay the void—and a massive black hole into which their companies' profits—and often, dissatisfied customers—were mysteriously disappearing. Who was in charge of their supply chains? How were goods tracked once they were in the system? Was there a system at all? More often than not, no one knew. Lost in space!

Next I saw that the typical delivery system-cum-black box was, in fact, a kind of plumbing system, with something—

goods—pumped in at one end, and something pumped out. Like a plumbing system, too, it also had valves, each of which could be adjusted in order to optimize output. As with a sink, the manager of the system—that is, you, the CEO, or the ultimate manager of the system—desires to put the minimum amount of water into the system, and have just the right amount of water pumped out at the right place. To be sure, no one really understood just how the valves of the system worked. Consequently many companies' delivery systems did not work. And, when the responsible supply chain or logistics managers tried to fix their systems they wound up applying band aids that did little or nothing to solve the problem.

Meditating on this logistical conundrum, I also perceived that this hypothetical delivery system could be modeled like an electronic circuit, in which I could measure the voltage at the beginning of the circuit, the end of the circuit, and anywhere in between.

I had taken three more steps along the road that would ultimately lead me to develop the Tri-Level View. I was almost there.

As you will see in the following section, in which I mark the steps I took in discovering the Tri-Level View, there will also be an epiphany-inducing packet of sugar in my future as well.

■ ■ ■ ■ ■

Meanwhile, through my wider reading, I had begun to better appreciate that the art of supply chain management, as applied in the business world, had come directly out of the experience of war and the challenge of finding and delivering *military* goods and materiel to the battlefield. I also discovered that some of history's Great Captains had been pretty good designers and businessmen—and logisticians—themselves. Section 1, *Supply and Command, A Journey through Time*, goes back in time in search of some of these imposing figures and looks at how they solved their battlefield logistical problems.

Logistics . . . What does it really mean? Where does it come from? What does it have to do with war? And what is the relationship between military logistics and business logistics? These are some of the questions answered in the next section, a historical walk across the shifting sands of time, in search of the Ultimate Logistician.

SECTION *I*

SUPPLY AND COMMAND, A JOURNEY THROUGH TIME

Chapter 1

War Is Logistics

"Without supplies, no army is brave."
—Frederick II of Prussia, in his
Instruction for his Generals, 1747

Military logistics was very much in the forefront of the mind of the Western world at the beginning of the 1990s as the United States, the United Kingdom, and its more than two dozen Coalition partners rampaged to victory in the short, blitzkrieg-like war known as Desert Storm, liberating Kuwait from Iraqi occupation. More than in any previous war, the media, taking their cue from the victorious commanding Coalition commander, General H. Norman Schwarzkopf, focused on the logistical skills of the winning side. Hitherto this was unknown territory for the modern-day press.

TV networks aired clips of the allies' combined formidable might that was deployed in Saudi Arabia—an astounding 670,000 men from 28 nations—while newspapers devoted considerable space to the vast numbers of soldiers, vehicles, and tonnages that were successfully moved to support them. After all, during the methodical six-month buildup prior to combat—Operation Desert Shield—the logistics of the operation was all there was to write about.

Most importantly and impressively, the massive logistic

preparations leading up to Desert Storm itself worked. Somehow the 150,000 troops of the U.S. VII and XVII Corps, with all their advanced weapons, ammunition, and supplies were able to secretly move 150 miles across the forbidding Arabian desert. In fact, most of their supplies were actually waiting for the troops when they got there! Simultaneously, the U.S. 82nd Airborne Division rampaged 250 miles across Iraq, with no hitch and with ample support. How?

Elementary, Schwarzkopf said, "Logistics."

Both at his famous press conferences and later in his memoirs, "Stormin' Norman" called Desert Storm a "logistician's war," handing much of the credit for the Coalition's lightning-swift victory to his chief logistician—or quartermaster general, as he would have been called in a previous era—Lieutenant General Gus Pagonis. Pagonis, Schwarzkopf declared, was an "Einstein who could make anything happen," and, in the Gulf War, did.

Likewise, media pundits from NBC's John Chancellor on down also attributed the successful result of the war to logistics.

What was *that* and what did it have to do with war?

Of course, logistics has everything to do with war. Indeed, as you will see, logistics *is* war, and the art of supply chain management derives directly from military logistics.

This explains why Lieutenant General Gus Pagonis, the logistical *wizard* behind the Allied success in Operation Desert Storm (as his boss, Norman Schwarzkopf called him) was able to readily adapt so many of the strategies and tactics he developed and used to move mountains for the U.S. Army to his subsequent and current position as vice president of logistics for Sears, Roebuck. Sears, Roebuck hired him directly from the military in 1991.

Fascinatingly, and revealingly, although Pagonis has been working in the civilian sector for over a decade, his main hero continues to be none other than his Greek ancestor, Alexander the

Great, who as we will see, inspired one of Pagonis's most effective logistical innovations, the mobile logbase. As he confirmed in his talks with me, his personal hall of fame also includes such logistically astute generals as Ulysses Grant and George Patton.

Why? And what do you as a forward-looking, innovative corporate planner or executive have to learn from these past figures? A lot, as you will see.

■■■■■

First, let us get our definitions straight. What exactly *is* logistics?

Definitions differ. In his authoritative book on military logistics, *Supplying War*, military historian Martin van Creveld defines logistics as "the practical art of moving armies and keeping them supplied." *Jane's Dictionary of Military Terms*, on the other hand, describes it as the art of "planning and carrying out the movement and maintenance of forces." Both definitions are valid.

So is the more comprehensive (if somewhat harder to chew) definition that Pagonis uses in his instructive memoir of the Gulf War, *Moving Mountains*. According to the former head of the U.S. Army's 22nd Support Command, military logistics equals the "transportation, supply, warehousing, maintenance, procurement, contracting and automation into [sic] a single function that ensures no suboptimization of those areas to allow the overall accomplishment of a particular strategy, objective, or mission."

In Chapter 4 of this section, we'll zoom in a little closer on Pagonis, who went on to brilliantly manage logistics for Sears, Roebuck. In addition to taking a closer look at Pagonis's historic achievement in Kuwait, we'll also talk with him about the surprisingly close relationship between military and business logistics.

Indeed, as we will see from Pagonis's example, as well as those of the many retired or former military logisticians who have applied their knowledge and skills to business logistics since World War II, business logistics is essentially an offshoot of military logistics. So it behooves us to look at the military side of the logistical coin first—besides the fact that the history and development of military logistics is a fascinating and important story unto itself. For, most popular literature about war notwithstanding, war is not just about tactics and strategy. The media and general public, not to mention many in the military itself, belatedly gleaned that in Kuwait. War is also, as General Schwarzkopf reminded America, very often about logistics.

■■■■■

Back to definitions. There is yet another, even more wide-sweeping, nonkhaki definition of logistics than Pagonis's quite comprehensive one that is *also* useful and valid in analyzing the broad sweep of military history. Successful military logistics can *also* mean the ability of the *entire* nation, or the national infrastructure and manufacturing base, to support its armed forces, much as America did during World War II, when American industry hearkened to President Roosevelt's call for the country to become "the arsenal of democracy."

In this sense, the greatest logistical hero of World War II was, arguably, a civilian, Henry Kaiser, the West Coast-based shipbuilder and manufacturing powerhouse who revolutionized the shipbuilding industry. Kaiser played a major role in winning the war through his extraordinary employment of mass prefabrication.

As John Keegan, the distinguished military historian, writes in his landmark book, *A History of Warfare*, "It was America's industry that overwhelmed its German and Japanese enemies, though only because American shipyards also supplied the transportation to move it."

Ultimately, more than 51,000,000 tons of merchant shipping was built by United States shipyards between 1941 and 1945, including some 10,000 Liberty and Victory freighters and T2 tankers. Kaiser's titanic shipyards in California and Oregon were responsible for nearly one-third of that output, as well as for building the most speedily built ships. When Kaiser, whose prior experience was in building dams and highways (he was such a landlubber that he called the bow of a ship "the front end"), first responded to the Allies' need for more tonnage, partly to replace the millions of tons sunk by Admiral Doenitz's happily marauding submarines, it took an average of 150 days to build a Liberty ship.

By the end of 1942, Kaiser's flying troupes of engineers and machinists were able to cut that time down to an astounding four days and fifteen hours and were turning out a ship *a day*, a rate Kaiser maintained until the end of the war, thus helping to win the crucial "Battle of the Atlantic." For four years the indefatigable builder—whose factories also turned out dozens of innovative and effective light, or jeep carriers—*was* the personification of the arsenal of democracy and of American logistical can-do.

In short, military logistics, especially modern-day military logistics, is not just a uniformed matter. General Pagonis may well have been the outstanding logistical hero of the Gulf War, but so were the men and women back home who made the equipment that he and the men and women under him then successfully managed to get to the battlefront itself.

■ ■ ■ ■ ■

However narrowly or broadly one defines the art of military logistics, it is hard to overestimate its importance in war. Logistics governs what units a nation's armed forces can deploy, the phasing of its war plans, as well as the selection of tactical objectives. Without logistics, war plans, quite simply, cannot be supplied, hence they cannot be executed.

To be sure, logistics isn't the *whole* game in war. As John Keegan, again, notes in *A History of Warfare,* "logistic supremacy on its own rarely wins a campaign against a determined enemy." Thus, the Union armies, which hapless General George McLellan led in the botched Peninsula Campaign of 1862, were better-supplied than their oft-bedraggled Confederate counterparts. However the Confederates were better led and better motivated, which is why McLellan was replaced later that year.

Fortunately, McLellan's replacement, Ulysses S. Grant, was a superior leader and tactician, not to mention a superior logistician. Later, after the tide of the Civil War had turned—thanks in part to Grant's brutal, logistic-minded, total-war strategy—and the South was even more bedraggled, its forces were still able to put up a formidable fight and occasionally win battles on the field. However, the South's utter logistical defeat, the near vitiation of its economy and war arsenal, meant that its total defeat was only a matter of time.

■■■■■

What, exactly, makes for a logistically astute and effective military commander?

According to P.D. Foxton, a career British logistics officer, and author of *Powering War: Modern Land Force Logistics*, these are the key traditional principles of effective military logistics: *foresight*, or the ability to plan and provide for one's forces' supply and transport on the battlefield, as well as to counter an opponent's logistics; *flexibility*, the ability to adapt logistical plans to dynamic battlefield conditions; *economy*, the ability to make most economical or efficient use of available materiel and supplies, including raw material; *simplicity*, the ability or talent to make logistic plans as simple as possible, and to clearly articulate them; and *cooperation*, the ability to secure the cooperation of one's allies or hosts in accomplishing the overall mission. Most of these principles can also be retroactively used as criteria for evaluating the logistic competence of the great captains or commanders of history.

Unsurprisingly, most, if not all, of the great commanders of military history have also been great, or at least competent logisticians. They had to be, in order to win. How consistently they managed their logistics is another matter.

Finally, I would add to the above one more crucial criterion for measuring logistical competence and greatness: *innovation*. As it happens, these are also effective criteria for evaluating the great captains of business, and how well and efficiently they run their logistics.

But first, using these criteria, let us go back two millennia and take a look at history's first great captain, Alexander the Great.

■■■■■

When, during the tense hours before Operation Desert Shield gave way to Operation Desert Storm, Norman Schwarzkopf asked his chief logistician upon what doctrine his logistical plan for the pending war was based, Schwarzkopf was somewhat taken aback by Gus Pagonis's reply. "I got the idea from a fellow Greek," the general-cum-military-history student replied with a straight face ". . . Alexander the Great."

Schwarzkopf, no mean student of military history himself, should not have been surprised by Pagonis's seemingly flip answer.

To be sure, in addition to being history's first great captain, Philip II, as he was originally known, was also its first logistician. Before he arrived on the world stage in the fourth century B.C. and unleashed his merciless phalanxes on his hapless Near Eastern and Asian neighbors, military leaders did not worry unduly about how to supply their small, usually close-range forces. When necessary, the four-legged supply trains attached to prehistoric armies could be supplemented by ad hoc plundering or foraging. Logistics—supply and transport—was not something to which the average early-day commander gave much considered thought.

However, Alexander's sweeping imperial ambitions put him into a new strategic, and thus logistic, league altogether. The brilliant, irrepressible, and somewhat mad (though no more than any of the other great megalomaniacs of history) Greek literally wished to conquer the world, and to a remarkable degree he possessed the logistical genius to fulfill his grandiose ambitions.

Indeed, as Donald Engels convincingly demonstrates in his 1977 book, *Alexander the Great and the Logistics of the Macedonian War*—the same monograph that Pagonis cites—logistics was at the heart of both Alexander's strategy and tactics for his 4,000-mile march from Egypt through Persia to India, the longest in history.

As Engels shows, few commanders-in-chief have given as much advance thought to their supply and transport problems as did Alexander. For his armies to be successful, he recognized from the start that they had to be as mobile as possible. This meant that they had to be as light as possible. The enormous impedimenta of his predecessors, with their cumbrous trains of wagons, women, and livestock, simply wouldn't do. Alexander wanted and needed a long range striking force that was lean and mean, and he got it.

As Frontinius, the Roman military historian, would later write with no little admiration, "When Alexander organized his first army he ordered that no one was to use a wagon. The horsemen he allowed one servant each, but for the infantry he permitted for every ten men one attendant only who was charged with carrying milling equipment and ropes."

Instead of the useless or hangers-on of yore, Alexander's highly sophisticated army was the first to employ specially trained engineers and quartermasters, in addition to cavalry and infantry. These primeval engineers played a crucial role in Alexander's early, successful efforts to reduce the fortified cities of Halicarnassus, Tyre, Gaza, and other citadels, as well as his later great marches. His able quartermasters, for their part, would administer the best logistics system of its day, and one that would endure to the twentieth century, inspiring future logisticians right up to Gus Pagonis.

Perhaps the most distinctive aspect of that system, and the one that Pagonis was most directly inspired by, was Alexander's invention and establishment of *advance* supply depots for his armies, to reinforce them as they advanced into enemy territory. To install this advance depot network, Alexander sent his representatives ahead of his troops with instructions to purchase food or forage in exchange for cash or the promise of payment after victory. Troop garrisons were then installed in order to oversee these forward supply dumps.

These advance provisioners had broad latitude of action. If the leaders or representatives in the territories Alexander intended to traverse and/or conquer and/or do battle on refused to allow such depots to be built, he simply instructed his men to take hostages to ensure that they were. Involuntary cooperation, you might call it, but it worked.

Thus established, these depots enabled Alexander's far-flung armies to hop from one depot—and one more or less easily annexed territory—to another. The savvy Greek also synchronized his advance with the harvest dates in the conquered or soon-to-be conquered countries. That's foresight. That's logistics.

Once underway, the economy-minded commander never took supplies for granted, often ordering a forced march in order to conserve his stores. Effective and vigilant control and command of the supply side of war, Alexander understood—as all the great captains of history have understood—was a prerequisite, if not *the* prerequisite for command and control of the battlefield itself.

Alexander was also the first military leader to work out the basic math behind supplying a large, expeditionary army. After considerable trial and error, Alexander and his military engineers calculated the effective tactical range of their phalanxes' force as no more than eight days from the point of supply, either by stationary or floating depot.

The distances and dimensions of Alexander's 4,000-mile march still boggle the mind. Thus, for Alexander's longest march from his home base, in 326 B.C., between the River Indus and the Markan in Baluchistan, a distance of 300 miles, he and his quartermasters managed to stockpile, by hook or crook, no less than 52,000 tons of provisions, sufficient to supply his sleek army of 87,000 infantry and 52,000 support crew during the four months they successfully operated in the region.

Because an animal train would have consumed its load, and the men would have eaten their individual allotments of thirty pounds of provisions well before the march was complete, he counted on the accompanying fleet to resupply his men as they marched near the Indian Ocean coast.

Alexander also expected the seasonal Asian monsoon to refresh the rivers from which his men would then take water at their estuaries. However, in this case, Alexander's carefully thought-out plans were undone by the fog of war. That fateful year—326 B.C.—the Asian monsoon blew in a different direction than it normally did. Instead of helping him, the monsoon hindered him, its winds confining his fleet to the mouth of the Indus, while his men died of thirst and starvation. Three-quarters of his men were lost. For all his foresight, Alexander had not been able to secure the cooperation of the gods.

Twenty-two hundred years later, in Normandy, an equally unexpected onslaught of monsoon weather created similar havoc with the invading Allied armies under General Dwight Eisenhower, severing their supply link to England, and depriving forward troops of supplies. There were fewer immediate casualties than Alexander's forces had suffered two millennia before in

Baluchistan, but the chaos on the beaches as well as further in-
land, as Eisenhower's and Montgomery's phalanxes ran short of
fuel and ammunition, temporarily halting their advance, was
nearly as fatal to the Allied advance as it was to Alexander's.

Fortunately, Ike's clever logisticians were able to improvise
their way out of the deadly logjam by jerry-rigging the motorized
Red Ball Express, a fleet of over 6,000 trucks, and the Allies'
bogged down battlewagon was able to move on.

Alexander's quartermasters were no less innovative. Unfortunately, they didn't have trucks. The weather gods won. But that
does not take anything away from his manifest genius as a commander, as well as his role as history's first logistician.

■■■■■

The next great logistician to emerge from the mists of ancient
military history was the redoubtable Carthaginian general, Hannibal. When the Second Punic War between Carthage and Rome
broke out in 218 B.C., this brave, bold, and innovative commander decided to take the fight to Italy. To do so, he used a novel
means of bringing his men and their supplies to the Mediterranean battlefront: the elephant truck.

Braving formidable difficulties and hardships, Hannibal led
his army of 60,000 stout-hearted men, backed up by 37 no less
stout-hearted elephants, across the Spanish Pyrenees, whereupon
his forces crossed the Rhone River over history's first pontoon
bridges, which had to be strong enough to bear the weight of
their baying elephant train, then across and through the Little St.
Bernard Pass into Italy; and finally onto three successive victories
over the Romans in two years—a remarkable combined feat of
arms and logistics.

In addition to being superb carriers of men and materiel,
Hannibal's African-imported elephant fleet also had the welcome
psychological side effect of scaring the living bejesus out of the

earthbound Roman troops, once they loomed into sight—although this advantage was dissipated once the no less frightened beasts ran amok in the ensuing battle.

In the end, Hannibal's inadequate logistics undid him. His lack of reinforcements or forward supply depots fatally weakened his expeditionary force, and the offensive threat they posed, allowing the Romans to recover from their initial surprise and to divert some of their stronger and better supplied forces to attacks upon Carthage itself. In 204 B.C. Hannibal was recalled, and in 202 B.C. he was decisively defeated by the Roman general Scipio Africanus (no mean commander himself) at Zama near his North African home base.

Eventually, under Roman pressure, the Carthaginians banished Hannibal, and the disgraced general fled to Crete. There, the still-enraged Romans pursued him, and rather than become their prisoner, he took his own life.

Nonetheless, Hannibal's amazing, elephant-borne foray through the Alps still stands out as one of the great masterpieces of logistical planning in military history.

Although it took a century or so for them to get the hang of it, the Romans and their generals certainly recognized the importance of supply and transport issues in creating, governing, and maintaining a great empire. That Julius Caesar was a great leader of men is well known. What is less well known is that he was also, like Alexander and Hannibal before him, a masterful and able logistician.

"I would prefer to conquer [my foe] by hunger rather than by steel," Caesar once said. He displayed his logistical acumen during the civil war against Pompeii, in which the cunning Pompeiians assayed the logistical-based strategy of starving out Caesar's army by setting fire to the adjoining fields (the first known use of scorched earth) and thereby forcing the army out of its blocking position atop the Ilerda plateau.

However, Caesar was prepared for such a contingency, having ensured that his men already had adequate rations before taking the heights. Instead of the Romans, it was the Pompeiians who wound up starving. Counterlogistics, you might call it.

Vegetius, perhaps history's first military theorist, placed considerable importance on logistics in his writings, urging, in one of his influential tracts, that "young soldiers must be given frequent practice in carrying loads of up to 60 pounds and marching along at the military pace, for on strenuous campaigns they will be faced with the necessity of carrying their rations as well as their arms."

After subsequent tests, the logistically minded Romans revised that figure somewhat, concluding that the maximum optimal load for an individual infantryman, or legion, was actually 70 pounds, half of which consisted of arms, clothing, and equipment, and the other half of food. If rations were consumed at the rate of three pounds a day, the army could march for 10 to 12 days before having to refit at one of the capacious supply depots that the Roman Senate wisely had installed every 16 miles.

Ultimately, of course, beyond the considerable impact and influence of either Caesar's generalship or Vegetius' writings on Rome's military fortunes, Rome's might was based squarely on its army itself, the world's first elite fighting force, whose superior discipline and weapons were the envy of their adversaries. Legions tended to be loyal to their own generals, and this support gave popular generals such as Caesar their real power. Power flowed from the bottom up.

Besides their outstanding discipline, esprit de corps, and weapons, the Roman army had something else their enemies were jealous of, and that was crucial to maintaining Rome's power: its far reaching, 10,000-mile network of chariot-tested, tough concrete roads. As John Keegan observes, "it was Rome's roads that made the legions who built them so effective an instrument of imperial power."

It was these, history's first highways, that enabled Roman commanders to calculate precise marching times between military storehouses and barracks, and between the outposts of its far flung empire. Thus, for example, they knew, because of their roads, that the march from Rome to, say, Brindisi, in order to quell unrest *there*, took precisely 15 days, whereas a march on Antioch, at the aforementioned rates of marching and food consumption, would take no less, and no more, than 124 days.

That was the working calculus behind the Roman Empire. *That* was logistics.

By the same token, once Rome's magnificent roads were allowed to decay, strategic planning was no longer possible, nor was Rome. Of course, hubris had something to do with the inevitable decline of the Roman empire, but so did logistics.

■■■■■

As other military historians have noted, the eight hundred or so years between the demise of the Roman Empire and the beginning of the Renaissance did little to advance the art of war or the art of military logistics. In addition, there were no great Western captains to speak of, with the possible exception of Charlemagne.

This lack of enlightened military leadership and of systematic logistics was especially evident in the numerous Crusades of the early centuries of the second millennium. The ill-led, ill-supported crusaders of the eleventh and twelfth centuries who tried to wrest control of Palestine from the Saracens and their Muslim brothers were often undermined and demoralized by their logistical incompetence. Faith alone, the crusaders found, was not sufficient to sustain them during the successive thousand-mile military expeditions to the Holy Land.

If the crusaders failed to appreciate the back, or logistical, side of the battlefield, their less starry-eyed enemies, especially the Turks, did. In the first successful use of scorched earth, the

Turks effectively stymied the Third Crusade, in 1078, by driving cattle off the crusaders' route as well as burning grass and even whole villages. Unfortunately for the hapless Christians, their otherwise fearless leader, Peter the Hermit, was considerably less clever than Caesar, who had earlier outwitted the Pompeiians when they had tried this gambit. The gambit worked. The hungry crusaders became a disorganized rabble. End of Crusade.

Logistics or, rather, the failure to give proper importance to logistics (in this case the need for paying for sealift ability), directly influenced the course of the fourth Crusade in 1096. Unable to pay the money-minded Venetians for their shipping, the rambunctious crusaders were persuaded by their leaders to sack the Christian city of Constantinople, which did little to endear them to the local populace.

Unfortunately, American Express traveler checks had not yet been invented. No crusader should leave home without them.

■ ■ ■ ■ ■

Meanwhile, from out of the East that redoubtable savage and formidable commander, Genghis Khan, had appeared with his Mongolian hordes to rape, pillage, and conquer.

At first blush, one would think that Genghis Khan would be the last one to give considered thought to logistical matters.

Actually, quite the opposite was true. Seen through the cold retrospective eye of history, Genghis was not only a brilliant tactician, cleverly separating his horsemen into tight columns before simultaneously converging on the hapless enemy from various directions; he was also a very able and resourceful logistician.

Ever keeping the logistical bottom-line in mind, Genghis instilled in his horsemen the importance of living frugally as well as *moving* frugally.

To help ensure the latter, the cunning Mongol had his mounted berserkers travel with three horses, one as primary mount, one to draw milk from, and a spare, which could also be eaten if necessary: logistics in motion.

Indeed, insofar as he pursued a deliberate strategy of killing civilians who were potential soldiers, as well as producers (i.e., decimating the opposing national arsenal at its source), one can argue that Genghis was the *ultimate* logistician.

The fewer bodies an adversary had, Genghis figured, the smaller the army he could raise, no less support.

Crude, yes, but the Khan's successes against the various twelfth century Western armies and peoples he faced speak for themselves. Consequently, he also deserves his own searing place in our military logistical hall of fame. Genghis schematized his supply chain and managed it in an expeditious, if brutal, way.

In a way, you could say, the Khan did have a Tri-Level View; he just lacked humanity. Then again, isn't the same true of many contemporary CEOs?

Chapter 2

To Forage or Not to Forage

"An army marches on its stomach."
—Napoleon Bonaparte

Sun Tzu, the great Chinese military theorist, was another Eastern warrior whose scruples do not stand up to modern scrutiny, as well as one who understood the importance of logistics to war. His much-quoted treatise, *The Art of War*, contains numerous rules and maxims on how to best support one's armies in the field, including very specific ones on how much and how often soldiers are to be paid. Logistics was clearly an important aspect of the art of war to Sun Tzu, and, evidently, to the ancient Chinese generals from whose operational experience he based his theories of warfare.

Ultimately, however, because of the enduringly *non*-logistic nature of the Chinese military tradition, the wisdom of Sun Tzu, particularly his logistical wisdom, would be honored more in the breach than in the practice by succeeding generations of Oriental warriors. That tradition, which continued up until and through the modern era, tended to feature sieges in which large massed armies attempted to invest large fortified towns.

The size of the challenge facing Chinese armies required

positive battlefield decisions to be achieved as swiftly as possible. With so many thousands of mouths to feed, siege logistics tended to be an improvised affair, disdaining rules or organization. Chinese generals were not so concerned with how to feed their men or how to support them over a period of time. They knew how to feed them: They just needed to get over those damned walls.

Instead of amassing food stores, Sun Tzu's descendents tended to be more concerned with amassing *bodies* than accumulating stores. Once the men had catapulted themselves over the walls, their leaders figured, they could get their own chow.

This is in direct contrast to the Western tradition of warfare, which tended, from medieval times forward, to become more and more protracted as the centuries wheeled on and vast conflicts ravaged the continent, thus requiring prolonged, well thought out support.

In this respect, the Thirty Years' War, from 1618 to 1648, was a watershed in the history and development of the art of military supply. The war was really a confused series of wars that began with a quarrel between the Protestant and Roman Catholic princes of Germany over who should become the next Holy Roman Emperor. It ultimately degenerated into a prolonged maelstrom involving France, Denmark, and Sweden in which the French somehow wound up fighting on the same side as the Protestant Netherlands, which was also a combatant in the fray.

What the commanders in that protracted war found, as their armies ballooned in size—and appetite—was that their sovereigns had raised more men than they could supply. The painful lesson of that messy, inconclusive conflagration, it became painfully evident to all, was that armies had to be kept within numbers that could be paid. Otherwise those same armies would become a disorganized, wanton rabble and alienate the local populace.

That might have been all right in the twelfth century, but it simply wouldn't do in the enlightened seventeenth century. Protracted warfare, along civilized lines, required rationality including—and especially—rational, *systemic* logistics.

Unsurprisingly, the civilization that most prided itself on its rationalism—the French—specifically the French father-and-son team of war administrators Michel and Louvois Le Tellier—came up with the dual system solution. Michel, the elder administrator, took the lead by calculating the ration requirements of an army, arranging for civilian contractors to supply food, and setting up a wagon train system with provision reserves. Meanwhile, son Louvois developed a new form of the magazine system, which had already been used since classical times, to ensure that frontier fortresses were well stocked with supplies that could be moved out to the armies by wagon or barge. Acknowledging the Le Telliers' genius, the French army quickly moved to adapt both systems. Problem solved!

Well, not quite.

If anything, the Le Telliers' system worked too well. The foraging problem was indeed solved but the army's renewed dependence on a wagon train reduced the army's mobility, hampering logistical and strategic fluidity. Under the new supposedly rational regime, armies were, of necessity, restricted to roads. That was fine as long as the roads were passable, but often, especially during the summer, they were not. Even when they were, the movement of armies was limited to marching within the region of the nearest magazine, which hindered planning. Thus, logistics became the master of strategy rather than its servant. The prior need for foraging, which had often led to looting and pillage, had been solved, but at the price of sacrificing mobility.

Also, although the French established a corps of *intendants* (as they were called) to supervise supply and expenditure, the new system still depended on contractors, who required payment, as well as upon civilian drivers, who were not proof against war's alarms.

Meanwhile, the supply needs of the typical European army

continued to mushroom. On average, the standing European army of the late seventeenth century numbered 60,000 troops, who needed 45 tons of bread a day—or the product of 60 portable bread ovens—and 200 wagon loads of fuel, amongst other things. In addition to this, there were the army's 40,000 horses, who needed 500 tons of fodder. Accumulating the latter, whether it was to be consumed on the spot or for storage in magazines, consumed time. Soldiers, pressed into vast foraging parties numbering in the hundreds, now spent more time wielding scythes than swords.

These fodder-gathering groups, usually commanded by lieutenant generals or other high-ranking officers, were generally more civilized about the way they went about their logistics business than their rapacious predecessors.

Well and good, but that was not the point, was it?

The point was to wage war—effectively, economically, and without alienating the local populace (and source of supply). The objective was, after all, to wage war, not to wage logistics.

Meanwhile, it had also become clear that continental armies, regardless of whether or not they used Le Tellier's magazine system, could no longer be supplied solely from the land. The effective, modern-day European commander also needed to be knowledgeable about river transport if he was to adequately supply and maintain his forces.

Winston Churchill's great ancestor, the Duke of Marlborough, understood this. Riverine transport was a main stay of the 1704 campaign against Germany in Bavaria, in which he successfully provided his troops by having supply-laden flat boats—the predecessor of World War II's LSTs—meet his 40,000 soldiers as they marched down the Rhine and then on to the Danube.

Three centuries later, Marlborough's near flawless Bavarian campaign is still considered one of his great set pieces of logistical planning, while the Duke himself still draws high marks from historians both for his logistics, as well as for the general professionalism of his men. Moreover, Marlborough, arguably the modern era's first truly professional commander, knew what all great commanders know: that an adequately fed, clothed, and otherwise supplied army was an effective army. Noel Coward, playing the part of a destroyer commander, would say the same thing to his sailors two centuries later in his famous, to-the-point, dockside speech before they set off for sea in the classic 1942 British war film, *In Which We Serve*: ". . . that a happy ship is an efficient ship and an efficient ship is a happy ship." Marlborough, at the helm of history's first truly professional army, ran the terrestrial equivalent of a happy, tight ship, and the triumphant results showed at Blenheim and elsewhere. One of his admirers declared, "The good order of his [Marlborough's] men, as well as the excellent condition of his horses were the direct result of his logistic genius."

History's next great captain, Frederick the Great, also took great care with his logistics. In 1743 the German leader set forth his philosophy of logistics thusly: "I would first conquer enough land to enable me to procure provisions, to live at the expense of the enemy, and to select as [my] theatre of operations, terrain that is most favorable to me."

George Washington, America's first great commander, also gave due weight to logistics, especially after the Revolutionary Army's first, beleaguered winter at Valley Forge. Of course, the revolutionary commander also had the very considerable advantage of playing on his own home court, so to speak. One of the principal reasons for the defeat of the British forces in the rebellious American colonies—and one which is often overlooked—was the great length of time required for replenishing the redcoats from their home base—or Zone of the Interior, as today's Army logisticians would call it—back in England, some three thousand miles away.

Which brings us to history's next great captain: Napoleon.

■■■■■

One might think that the author of perhaps military history's best-known maxim on logistics—that "an army marches on its stomach"—not to mention one of the greatest warriors of all time, was also a master logistician.

In truth, though, seen over the course of his military career and conquest, the Great One, as Napoleon Bonaparte was called in his day, actually managed his logistics rather poorly.

On the plus side, Napoleon did revise the system of semi-organized foraging which his Revolutionary predecessors had introduced. He also was sufficiently logistics-minded to include food stuffs amongst the items he required his intelligence service to gather data on. An admirer of Marlborough's logistics, he likewise arranged for supplies to be stored in enemy areas in advance of his troops. As a logistician, he could also be innovative. Witness his use of hard tack instead of fresh bread, of which he tried to make certain his troops had several days' supply. As his armies advanced, his agents patiently scoured the countryside for food. All this redounds to Napoleon's credit.

Napoleon's early campaigns included several logistical set pieces—most notably the movement of his army from Boulogne to Austerlitz in 1805, which called for intricate planning and transport arrangements in order to overcome the advantage enjoyed by the opposing Austrians and Russians by dint of proximity to their bases. In emulation of Marlborough, he also arranged for several hundred supply wagons to be sent ahead. Unfortunately, the wagons were sent to the wrong place. Wisely, like Marlborough, Napoleon replaced these with more efficient German ones, with happier results.

The brilliant *manoeuvre sur les derriers* Napoleon performed at Ulm, also in 1805, was a similar feat. Such was the Corsican troops' *esprit de corps* that they were happy to maintain the breakneck, 16-to-19-mile-an-hour pace the maneuver required, even though they were not properly nourished. In this instance, Napoleon's highly motivated men, contradicting his own maxim, soldiered on despite their gnawing stomachs, rather than waiting to fill them, and they were happy to do so. As one dedicated *grognard* wrote in his journal: "We have to make do without bread, but we make do anyway!"

Indeed, as his early conquests in Central Europe clearly demonstrated, no one lived off the land as well as Napoleon—when, in fact, there was adequate land to live off of.

Napoleon also demonstrated his appreciation for the importance of logistics by elevating Louis-Alexandre Berthier, the former *marechal de logis* to the position of chief of staff. Supply troops were also organized into a separate corps, the *Intendant*, which helped rationalize what was, at heart, an ad hoc process.

Indeed, all went well for Napoleon, logistically, as long as the *Intendant* had adequate stores to requisition. In Austria and Germany, where there was an ample harvest and local resources were extensive, he found to his satisfaction, his men could both make do *and* make time.

But in a poor region, large armies that attempted to live off the land ran the risk of alienating the local citizenry by depriving them of their scarce stores, especially if the armies were domiciled in the area for a long period. That is exactly what happened in Spain from 1805 to 1809, where Napoleon's forces made do for four years and wound up creating fierce resistance amongst the local populace.

Napoleon's essentially improvisational logistical strategy continued to backfire on him in Poland, in 1809, after his army's initial victories in the western part of that country. All was well as long as the men moved and foraged in the excellent agricultural country east of the Vistula. However, when they crossed that river and the weather changed, the system for feeding them collapsed.

Napoleon also continued to be plagued by the poor quality of his quartermasters. Although Berthier, his amanuensis, did his best to staff the corps with good officers, the job of supply and maintenance carried no special esteem in Napoleon's army, and the lower echelons of the supply corps were generally manned with bottom-of-the-barrel men who had no qualms about pillaging and plundering.

The principal fault, however, lay with Napoleon himself. Never all that interested in logistics to begin with, Napoleon—like Hitler, another indifferent logistician—became even less interested in the subject as the Napoleonic Wars of the first two decades of the nineteenth century rolled on and he became more and more absorbed with achieving his grand plan of conquest. Inevitably, this indifference—this fundamental impracticality in the man—was transmitted downwards, with fateful results.

In 1812, Napoleon belatedly realized his logistic sloppiness and tried to correct it before he ordered his men to march on Moscow. Wisely he organized a limited magazine system, setting up supply depots with biscuits, flour, oats, and spirits for his troops. He also increased the size of his train service to 26 battalions, 8 of which were equipped with 600 light and medium vehicles, while others were equipped with no less than 252 four-horse wagons, each capable of carrying one-and-a-half tons of grain and fodder. The invaders, numbering over 400,000 at the start, also brought with them 60,000 spare horses.

In the end, as David Moore, co-director of Britain's Cranfield University's Acquisitions and Logistics Unit, has noted, "Napoleon failed the logistics test [as soon as] he crossed the Nieman to start his Russian campaign." The Polish roads Napoleon's men traversed en route to their Russian debacle were not able to handle the load of the heavier wagons. Lighter wagons on the other hand, would have required even more horses, and, neither the too-few-and-far-between magazines nor the frost-laden invaded regions were able to provide enough fodder for the beasts who began to starve shortly after they entered Russia, followed soon by the men themselves. By the time they reached Moscow, following their defeat by Russian forces, the Emperors' hard-put men were down to 100,000, excluding stragglers. "The battle of Borodino only partly explains the shortfall," Moore continues, in his searing indictment of Napoleon's logistics. "He [Napoleon] had known [his] logistics system would not sustain his army on the road to Moscow and keep it there. He gambled that he could force the Russians to the negotiating table and dictate terms. He failed, and so had to retreat, a venture which logistic breakdown (as much as the weather or Russian pursuit) turned into a rout. . . ."

Of course, Napoleon's plan of conquest itself was flawed. Fatally, he underestimated Mother Russia, including the harsh Russian winters; Hitler would make the same mistake 130 years later.

However, unquestionably, Napoleon was also undermined by his botched logistics. If the French dictator had possessed the logistical foresight of Alexander the Great, no less his equally megalomaniacal but more practical predecessor's flexibility and economy, his ill-judged Russian venture just may have been successful.

■■■■■

Napoleon's esteemed counterpart and frequent nemesis, the British Duke of Wellington, certainly cared about logistics, and managed them consistently and well. "Strategic and military operations depend upon supplies," the great English general wrote in 1809, while he was stationed in India. "There is no difficulty in fighting, and in finding the means of beating your enemy," he wrote. "But to gain your objects, you must feed."

Wellington—who, as a regimental commander, had seen first hand the fatal consequence of slipshod supply and maintenance during the disastrous British invasion of the Low Countries in 1794—was, in fact, obsessed with logistics. If Napoleon dreamed of conquest, Wellington dreamed of oxen or bollocks, as they were called then. "Good movement cannot be made without good cattle, well-driven and well-taken care of," he wrote in 1810.

Wellington's logistic-mindedness was duly transmitted to his lieutenants. It was said that Wellington's only requirement of his lieutenants was that they be brave. Untrue. He also required them to care, as he did, about bollocks and about logistics in general.

As the current British Chief of Staff, General Charles Guthrie, recently wrote in an encomium to his illustrious predecessor in *The Daily Telegraph*, "Today's Army owes him [Wellington] much. He introduced the division as a fighting formation that had a mix of troops and weapons and could sustain itself and fight on its own." Turning to Wellington's logistical legacy, Guthrie continues, "[Wellington] changed the supply system and wagon train from which today's Royal Logistics Corps [the branch of the British Army that oversees logistics] is descended. It has been said of him that 'he wished to be able to trace a biscuit from Lisbon to a man's mouth in the frontier.'"

Wellington's quartermaster in Spain, Archibald Murray, arguably military history's most powerful quartermaster—at least until Gus Pagonis in the Gulf War—was responsible for the issuance of orders for all types of movement in both the front of the battlefield, as well as in the rear areas, including intelligence gathering and map making. And, unlike his oft-hard-pressed counterpart, Berthier, his commander-in-chief saw to it that he had good men under him.

The logistic-minded Duke also saw to it that his provisioners in foreign lands had something else that came in handy: cash, with which his quartermasters were able to set up market and purchase their supplies, and which he found much preferable to foraging. The locals tended to like it better, too.

Finally, too, his logistical plans were simple in concept, as well as simple to understand. Thus, Wellington compared the two main elements of his plan for supplying his troops during the Peninsular War of 1807–1814—sea and road transport—to

that of a rope. If snapped, he would simply tie the two pieces together and continue.

Indeed, by all of the aforementioned criteria for a great commander who *also* was a great logistician, Wellington passes with
flying colors.

■ ■ ■ ■ ■

The American Civil War was, in many ways, the first total war, insofar as it pitted two sides against each other—the North and the
South—each determined, with large populations from which to
draw recruits and large arsenals to supply them. This laid the
foundation, at the onset of hostilities in February, 1861, for a
long war, one that would not be determined by one or two battles
but by campaigns, whose outcome would be determined by the
respective powers of the opponents' arsenals, and the ability of
the respective economies to sustain a long war. Therefore, strategy had to take into consideration not only the combatants' own
logistical requirements, but also those of the enemy.

As such, each side, if it desired to win, needed a commander
who, in addition to being a master strategist and tactician, also
was a superb logistician. George McClellan, the first Union commander, clearly was not up to the job, as he demonstrated during
the disastrous Peninsular campaign that dominated the first year
of the war, from 1861 to 1862, when he allowed Southern forces
to come within striking distance of the Capitol itself.

Like most of the starting line-up on both sides, the debonair
McClellan did not understand the full dimensions of the conflict.
He did not understand the proper use of technology's newest gift
to war, the railroad, either, as he demonstrated in Virginia, where
the logistically-challenged general's initial failed strategy showed
the danger of becoming *too* dependent on railways for supplies.
And, too, he lacked something else: a killer instinct.

Fortunately for the Union cause, McClellan's successor,

Ulysses S. Grant, was everything that the charming, hapless McClellan was not. Woefully uncharismatic, given to troublesome dark moods and, sometimes, drunken binges, this unprepossessing veteran of the Mexican War quickly proved himself the man of the hour once he took the reins of the Northern armies from the man who briefly replaced McClellan, the equally inadequate Ambrose Burnside, in early 1863. A master strategist, thoroughly committed to the Union cause, Grant, who had already displayed his considerable military acumen during the first two years of the war, quickly demonstrated that he understood both the complexity and the gravity of the challenge he had been handed, and was committed to seeing the job of defeating the Confederates to the end, come hell or high water.

Although much has been written about Grant's superior generalship, little attention has been given to his superb logistics. A one time supply officer, Grant clearly understood the transport dimension of warfare, including both river and railway transport. His riverine skills were certainly on a par with those of his illustrious, logistically minded predecessors, the dukes of Marlborough and Wellington. Indeed, as John Keegan has observed, it was Grant's facile use and understanding of waterways as a strategic pivot that first brought him to the attention of the hard-pressed Union CEO, Abraham Lincoln.

Grant also understood a thing or two about railroads. Indeed, his crucial victory at Chatanooga, in November 1862, derived its principal significance from the severance of the Chatanooga-Atlanta rail link, the track connecting the Confederate system west and east of the Appalachian mountain chain, thus enabling him to cut off the South's distribution network for grain and meat from Mississippi to Richmond. Even before that, while operating along the river lines of the Cumberland and Mississippi, Grant, the logistician, had shown that he understood how the railroad could be used as a subsidiary means to strategic and even tactical mobility.

Thus, during the 1862 Vicksburg campaign, Grant successfully used the railroad network as an ancillary to the Mississippi, moving, as he put it in his directive, "One or sometimes two corps at a time to reach designated points out parallel to the railroad and only six to ten miles from their point of supply," a highly sophisticated technique ensuring that his trains of mules and horse-drawn wagons didn't operate more than a single day's march from their point of bulk loading. Unlike Alexander's—and Wellington's—animal-train columns, they, therefore, consumed none of their own loads and were no more tired out by their work than the dray horses of the milk trucks that plodded the streets of mid-nineteenth century America.

As John Keegan, a great admirer of Grant, also notes in his book *History of Warfare*, Grant's correspondence is full of strict, often ruthless instructions about how railroads—which stood high on his index of what he felt made warfare "progressive"— ought to be used. Thus, for example, on January 3, 1863, six months before the pivotal Union victory at Gettysburg, he instructed a divisional commander on the necessity of keeping the Memphis and Charleston Railroad open. "It is my determination to run the road as long as we require it and *if necessary I will remove every family from between the Hatchie and Cold Water Rivers* [my italics]. For every raid or attempted raid by guerrillas upon the road," he coolly declared, "I want ten families of the most noted secessionists sent south." Grant was equally emphatic in his orders regarding the destruction of Confederate railways. "Burn up the remainder of Black River [railway] Bridge," he wrote to another subaltern later that spring. "Pile up ties and lay the rails across them and burn them up." Here was a general who put a premium on transport, to say the least.

To be sure, in his own slightly more civilized way, Grant's cold-blooded strategic-cum-logistic vision bears more than a slight resemblance to that of our old friend and ultimate logistician, Genghis Khan. Unlike Khan, Grant stopped short of deliberately erasing the civilian population of the rebel regions he operated in—but only just. However he had no compunctions whatsoever about denying the enemy the means to feed himself or his armies. Indeed, Grant's entire strategy, once he went over to the offensive—a strategy that the gentlemanly commander of the Rebel armies, Robert E. Lee, never seemed quite able to grasp or counter, perhaps because its essential amorality was so foreign to him—was to defeat the South by depriving it both of future recruits and its agriculture and industry.

To Grant, extremism in the defense of Union and liberty—to paraphrase the late Barry Goldwater—was defensible.

However, as Keegan also notes, Grant's real originality as a great captain-cum-logistician was shown later in that same momentous year of 1863, when, in a logistically inspired move the Union commander decided to, in his words, "cut loose altogether from my base and move my whole army without a rear link," utterly dispensing with what today's logisticians would call his Rear Logistics Area.

Put another way, Grant decided to forage. Previously, as we have seen, Napoleon had made foraging, or requisitioning, the principal basis for supplying his armies in Spain and elsewhere, with decidedly mixed results. However, this age-old logistical technique had never been tried in a country as productive as the Confederate states.

Grant's ingenuity produced remarkable results. "I was amazed at the quantity of supplies the country afforded," he wrote to one of his subalterns in 1862. "It showed that we have subsisted off the country for two months instead of two weeks without going beyond the limits designated. This taught me a lesson which was taken advantage of later in the campaign when our army lived twenty days with the issue of only seven days' supply by the commissary."

Meanwhile, Grant, in accord with his basic, counter-logistical strategy for defeating the South, continued to deny the Rebels what they wanted for themselves. In 1862 he had already forced southern civilians, starving in an area he had laid bare, to emigrate east or west, 15 miles and make do with what was left. During the siege of Vicksburg, as he recalled in his memoirs, he sent his subordinate, General Blass, into the surrounding neighborhood, which was "rich and full of supplies, both food and forage [sic]. He was instructed to take all of it. The cattle were to be driven in for use of our army, the food and forage to be consumed by our troops or destroyed by fire."

To be sure, as Keegan points out, similar tactics had been used before by Grant's predecessors, including the Duke of Marlborough, who had laid waste to Bavaria in 1704. But Marlborough's objective then had been to provoke battle with the French. Grant's aim in 1863, when he turned to advanced counterlogistics—or scorched earth—was more basic: to destroy the enemy's ability to eat and, not so incidentally, his ability to procreate. Starving Rebel women, he figured, were less likely to make Rebel babies.

"Rebellion," Grant wrote to one of his division commanders in April 1863, "has assumed that shape now that it can only be terminated by the complete subjugation of the south or the overthrow of the government," a prospect which, even after the Confederates' defeat at Gettysburg, still seemed unlikely. "It is our duty therefore to use every means to weaken the enemy by destroying their means of cultivating their field." In this effort, Grant sought to enlist the aid of the newly emancipated slave population. "You will encourage all Negroes, particularly middle aged males, to come within our lines [and] destroy or bring off all the corn and beef cattle you possibly can," he bluntly ordered.

Foresight, flexibility, economy, innovation—Grant's general-ship and ability as a logistician displayed all these qualities, combined with a frightening killer instinct. Clearly, a man you wanted to have on your side if you were involved in putting down a nasty civil war. Cooperation? No, Grant didn't give a fig about cooperation, a principle that, perforce, becomes dispensable when dealing with a determined insurrection.

Over a longer period, Grant's ruthless and indeed cruel counterlogistic, starve-the-enemy strategy and tactics might have cost him public support in the North—if the war had been allowed to go much beyond the already-exhausting point that it did. But it didn't. In any case, as he must have anticipated, that cold-blooded strategy, which ultimately brought the South to its knees—even while its men continued to fight with élan in the field—did make him a figure of hatred in the South. Grant was able to assuage some of that hatred by his generous and nonvindictive policy towards the Confederacy after his noble opponent, Robert E. Lee, finally sued for peace at Appomattox Court House in April 1865, when, to Lee's surprise, Grant told him that his soldiers could keep their weapons, as well as later, when Grant was elected president himself.

William Tecumseh Sherman, Grant's disciple and eventual successor as commander-in-chief of the United States Army, however, continued to be loathed by his vanquished opponents. Initially alarmed by Grant's strategy of baseless campaigning and scorched-earth tactics, Sherman wound up taking that philosophy of war to its extreme with the brutal campaign he launched from Atlanta in 1864, better known as Sherman's March. Ordering Atlanta to be leveled after his departure, Sherman advanced with his four army corps in parallel lines across a 50-mile front, destroying railways and living off the land with a vengeance, harrowing events, which, 75 years later, would be immortalized in the Hollywood epic, *Gone With the Wind*. Who can forget the scene in which Vivien Leigh's Scarlett O'Hara shoots the barbarous Union looters who had invaded her precious house, Tara?

Those barbarians were Sherman's men, and Grant's as well.

Nevertheless, although Grant's logistics, like Genghis Khan's, were not for the squeamish, he does fulfill, with one key exception, cooperation—our definition of a logistically astute commander-in-chief. He had foresight. He was flexible. He was resourceful. His plans were simple. And they generally worked.

The fact is, as we have seen, because they perceive their needs and how to obtain them more clearly than most, barbarians often make the damnedest logisticians.

■ ■ ■ ■ ■

And, of course, those barbarians were Lincoln's men, too. Indeed, Sherman's March can be well construed as the logical outcome of Lincoln's own unforgiving definition of secession as a criminal act by individuals, rather than a war waged by a sovereign, civilized state, and which, therefore, ought to be conducted along civilized lines.

Indeed Lincoln was demonstrably pleased when, at the conclusion of Sherman's March, Sherman "made a present to" him, as he put it, of the port of Savannah, along with 150 captured guns and 250,000 bales of cotton. Well done, Lincoln said, well done.

In this case, who can we say was the ultimate logistician, Grant or Sherman? It is difficult to say. One suspects that Alexander, not to mention Genghis Khan, would have approved of both, even if the latter probably would not have understood the ideal—the preservation of the United States—which originally drew both men to the colors as well as to such ruthlessness.

Meanwhile, Sherman remains a hated figure in the South to this day, and any Yankee who dares to whistle his berserkers' infamous song, "Marching through Georgia," even in jest, is taking his life into his hands.

Not that Sherman would have minded the opprobrium. "War is cruelty," he declared, in answer to his contemporary critics. "The crueler it is, the sooner it is over."

Questionable ethics, perhaps, but certainly sound logistics.

Chapter 3

The Arsenal
of Democracy

"In the emergency of war our nation's powers are
unbelievable."
—Ernie Pyle, the great World War II correspondent

It took a while, but by the end of the nineteenth century most of
the major Western powers had come to recognize that logistics
was just as important to waging war as strategy and tactics, and
that sometimes—especially in the hands of a supply-minded
commander like Grant—good logistics could make the difference
between victory and defeat. At the same time, as the requirements of modern war evolved, it also became increasingly clear
that the power and breadth of opponents' arsenals were just as
important as, if not more important than, the logistical expertise
of individual commanders in the field.

World War I was perhaps the first war to demonstrate the relative value of generalship, while illustrating the increasing importance of logistics in the most comprehensive sense of the word.

Total wars such as World Wars I and II depended above all
on *mass*, which, perhaps not surprisingly, led directly to a philosophy of logistics called *mass logistics*, the gist of which was
that if your national arsenal produced enough materiel and if

you got enough of it onto the battlefield in reasonable time, you would probably win.

However, as we shall see, this crude philosophy, which tended to de-emphasize the importance of tactics or even strategy, had mixed blessings both for the military and the civilian economy, where the residue penetrated the postwar business world's thinking about physical distribution.

But we are getting ahead of ourselves.

Accurately called the War to End All Wars, World War I, which lasted from 1914 to 1918, was war truly unlike anything that had preceded it. So were its logistics. (Not only did the opposing armies and their commanders, particularly the German army at the beginning, outstrip their logistics systems with the amount of men, equipment, and horses moving at a fast pace, but they totally underestimated their ammunition requirements, particularly for artillery.) Once the war became trench bound, as it quickly did, supplies were also needed to build fortifications that stretched along the whole of the Western Front.

Adding to this maelstrom was the need to build up for and husband supplies for the incessant, bloody, massive, and usually pointless attacks across the muddy No Man's Land that separated both sides. Given this, little wonder that the war dragged on at such a snail's pace.

The bottom line was that the arsenals of the Allies—the British, the French, and the Russians, until they withdrew from the war following the Russian Revolution in 1917—and their German and Austrian opponents were relatively evenly matched. The inevitable result: stalemate.

It was not until 1918 that the British, learning the lessons of the previous four years, and with more competent leaders in charge—although neither side boasted anyone who could be called a great commander, or anything approaching it—showed how an offensive ought to be carried out, with supply tanks and motorized gun sledges helping to maintain the pace of the advance, and to maintain supply well away from the railheads, where supply dumps could not be blasted by long-range artillery. It was no longer true to say that supply was easier when armies kept on the move. After 1914, as a result of the amount of ammunition the armies needed, and the expansion of transport required to lift the materiel and other supplies forward to its consumers—that is, the front-line soldiers—who needed it, the reverse applied.

Meanwhile, the long, drawn-out, nihilistic conflict had seen the introduction of technology's next great gift to military logistics: the internal combustion engine. The new warhorse, the truck, was to play a key role in World War I once it was introduced in 1915. During the defense of Verdun in 1916, the French employed no less than 2,500 trucks to transport an average of 13,000 men, along with nearly 2,000 tons of stores daily over a distance of 85 miles, a remarkable rate which they were able to maintain for nearly a month. Verdun was held; the conflagration slogged on.

Nevertheless, as Martin van Creveld, the pre-eminent historian of military logistics, asserts in his seminal study, *Supplying War*, neither the Allies nor the Germans possessed the imagination to take full advantage of this remarkable advance in warfare. "The problems encountered by the [Allied] motor transport companies as they struggled to maintain the flow of ammunition are interesting," he writes, "because they are typical of an army which, though, standing on the threshold of a new mechanical age, had not yet adapted either its instruments of control or its thought-processes to the newly acquired technical means . . . Important as they were, the motor transport companies were utilized inefficiently, and could not adapt themselves to the rapidly changing tactical situation."

Of course, if a flexible, innovative, and logistically astute commander, like an Alexander or a Marlborough or a Grant had been present to help speed up those thought processes, it might have been a different story. Instead, the Allies were saddled with stunted, disengaged commanders like Douglas Haig and Marshal Foch, with no feeling for either the human or materiel resources at their command; fortunately, Kaiser's equally challenged commanders were not much better. And so, for the better part of the war, the two sides simply threw millions of men, along with millions of tons of materiel, at each other, until, by 1918, each had virtually exhausted the other.

To be sure, World War I did not lack its own logistic set pieces, particularly beyond the stalemated Western Front. (The otherwise misguided Gallipoli operation of 1915, in which British and French forces unsuccessfully tried to force the Dardanelles against the Turkish defenders nevertheless did demonstrate how a navy could support an army with amphibious landing craft without ports—a lesson that, we shall see, D-Day planners in the next war did not heed sufficiently.)

The Palestine campaign of 1916–1918 "was a masterpiece of logistic planning," according to Joseph Sinclair, author of *Arteries of War: A History of Military Transportation*, with its brilliant combined use of a 140-mile standard gauge railway and a 12-inch water pipeline built from the Suez Canal across the Sinai Desert, as well as some local friends. In that remarkable, now all-but-forgotten campaign, water was transported to the army from the head of the pipeline at Beersheba by means of 35,000 camels, "thus . . . combining ancient transportation methods with the wonders of modern technology."

In the end, these were simply sideshows to the main, blood-drenched show of the Western Front, where the stalemate was finally broken, not by the use of superior strategy or tactics or logistics, but from the infusion of new bodies and fresh blood; in this case, the new bodies and fresh blood were the American Expeditionary Force that came to the weary Allies' aid in February, 1918. In this sense, World War I, unlike the Civil War or the world war that followed, was, ultimately, not a war of logistics, but simply a war of numbers. If the Germans had half a million fresh soldiers instead of the Allies, they might have won, too.

■■■■■

As in World War I, the combined arsenals of the opposing Allied and Axis powers were, roughly, evenly matched at the start of World War II, and continued to be until the entry of the United States. However, once the United States became a combatant following the surprise attack at Pearl Harbor, and the unmatched American manufacturing base was fully mobilized—a complex process that took another year and a half to fully complete—and given the absolute moral commitment of the Allies and their leaders *to win*, an element that had been missing in the nonideological Great War that preceded it, there was little question about the ultimate outcome.

The fact that the Allies, in this case, were *also blessed* with a number of gifted political leaders to guide their nations and armies to victory was, of course, also a welcome new factor. These leaders included Franklin Roosevelt, Winston Churchill, and, in this sense it must also be said, Joseph Stalin, as well as an array of superior theater commanders, including, most notably, Dwight D. Eisenhower, Douglas MacArthur, and Georgi Zhukov, who, in turn, were backed up by an equally impressive complement of army and corps commanders, including Bernard Montgomery, George S. Patton, Bernard Slim, and others.

How good were these generals as logisticians? Upon reflection, the logistic expertise of the individual commanders varied greatly. However, that tended to matter less than the unparalleled size and breadth of the Allied arsenal itself. Once the sleeping American giant was awakened, to paraphrase General Yamamoto, the architect of the attack on Pearl Harbor, once America's massive industrial power—in conjunction with the commitment of the American people to fight the war to its finish—was harnessed to the war effort, there really was no stopping it. In this sense, the conflict was indeed very much a war of logistics.

In retrospect, the dimensions of the American industrial and economic mobilization during World War II still stagger the mind. It wasn't just the boys on the front line, brave though they were, who made a maximum effort. The whole country did. As a result, between 1941 and 1945 the Gross National Product increased by 50 percent. Spearheaded by that American pharaoh, Henry J. Kaiser, the domestic shipbuilding industry, taking up FDR's initial challenge to make America the arsenal of democracy, increased its capacity by an astounding 1,000 percent. The aircraft industry even bettered that slightly, expanding capacity to 1,100 percent.

The first place where the might of the American arsenal was felt and made a difference was in the Battle of the Atlantic, when, beginning in mid-1943, the massive numbers of Liberty ships and other cargo ships that the United States was able to put into the water began to offset the ones that the German U-boat wolf packs were sinking, in the so-called tonnage war, so that our English and Russian allies could be supplied. In his memoirs, Churchill later claimed that this maritime battle of supply was the only aspect of the war that ever caused him to truly lose sleep. Improved antisubmarine tactics, combined with long-range fighter aircraft that could afford better protection to Allied ship convoys helped clinch this battle, but it was the sheer numbers of boats—ultimately over 10,000—that American shipyard workers built and launched that truly turned the tide in this new, altogether different battle, which was also a logistic set piece.

Soon, too, the effect of the no-less astounding numbers of aircraft launched by American factories—over 300,000 by war's end—also began to be seen and felt over the skies of occupied Europe, as the mighty Eighth Force launched massive bombing raids, some involving over one thousand bombers at a time, against Nazi Germany's heartland, including its sources of supply.

The first wave of these raids, in the fall of 1943, had indifferent results and caused unacceptably high levels of casualties amongst the air force crews. The most infamous of these was directed against the German ball-bearing manufacturing plants at Schweinfurt and resulted in the loss of nearly 200 bombers and their crews, out of a strike force of 1,100—nearly a 20 percent loss rate. This led the American high command to temporarily suspend long-range daylight raids, at least until long-range fighter escort could become available. Once such support did become available, in the welcome form of hundreds of spanking new P-40 fighters, in early 1944, the raids resumed, with telling effect. Beginning in 1944, successful bombing raids were also directed against the railway and highway system of occupied France, as part of the preparation for the invasion of Fortress Europe later that spring.

■■■■■

As far as D-Day itself is concerned, it does not take anything away from this greatest and most successful amphibious invasion in the history of warfare to say that it was also a logistical debacle, or nearly so. Indeed, an objective analysis of the logistical planning for what became known as The Longest Day only serves to emphasize its stature as a feat of arms, because the logistics and logistical thinking behind the mammoth operation, and the breakout of Allied armies after that, were so outstandingly poor.

As Martin van Creveld notes in *Supplying War*, D-Day's botched logistics began in London, during the planning stages. For one thing, there were too many planners. By November, 1943, eight months before D-Day, as van Creveld records, there were no less than 562 officers and men engaged in planning the supply and transport aspects of the invasion, with personnel divided between a rear and forward headquarters, who, in turn, required their own rapid courier service in order to communicate with each other. Consequently, "the 1944 army resembled a Brontosaurus, except that in the case of the latter day monster, the brain was large out of all proportion with the body, instead of vice versa."

Not surprisingly, the plan created by this creature was overly complex, involving artificial harbors and other unworkable innovations, which, during the invasion wound up cluttering the landing beaches and increasing the danger to shipping, and generally causing chaos that increased with the onset of monsoon weather on D-Day plus 20.

The subsequent havoc is recreated in alarming detail in *A Soldier Supporting Soldiers*, the memoirs of Joseph Heiser, who began his career in military logistics as a planner at Supreme Headquarters Allied Expeditionary Force (SHAEF) and eventually rose to become the Army's top logistician during the Vietnam War. Reluctant to name names, Heiser is not shy about recalling the dark (i.e., logistical) side of D-Day. In his little-known but eye-opening book, we see overwrought commanders desperately searching for the 81 mm. shells they needed for fighting in the Normandy hedgerows; entire ammo trains destined for one army winding up in the wrong army; and generals returning to England to find entire regiments they had somehow lost in the confused melee that occurred on and around the invasion beaches.

Once the breakout from the Normandy beachhead was achieved, thanks to the bravery, resolve, and sheer guts of the troops who had been embarked as well as the key support provided by the U.S. Navy, the planners back at SHAEF took on the role of a collective doubting Thomas, telling commanders, in effect, that they could not do what they were already doing.

Thus, as van Creveld observes, the SHAEF logisticians' feasibility study of August 11, 1944, two months following D-Day "showed that if a whole series of conditions was met it might be possible to support a tentative offensive by four U.S. divisions across the Seine on September 7. This conclusion, however, was further qualified by their recommendation that Allied operations south of the Seine ought to be halted in favor of an attack on the [English] Channel ports, and that the liberation of Paris should be postponed until late October when railways from the Normandy area would hopefully be available to carry relief supplies."

In fact, SHAEF notwithstanding, Paris was liberated on August 25, 1944, and by the target date of September 7, the U.S. Third Army had already penetrated two hundred miles beyond the Seine!

That's because its hell-bent-for-leather commander refused to be tied down by the hidebound headquarters logisticians' too-conservative tables.

That bold, thrusting, pearl-handled-revolver toting commander, of course, was none other than Lieutenant General George S. Patton. Such was Patton's indifference to and contempt for logisticians in general that throughout the entire 1944–1945 European campaign, he only saw his G-4, or chief supply officer, a total of two times: once before he assumed command of the Third Army in August, and the next and final time nine months later, in May, 1945, just before the war in Europe ended.

In between those dates, Patton essentially acted as his own supply officer. As Heiser, still shocked at the memory, recalls, Patton was an avid poacher of supplies—from his own side. "At one point," Heiser remembers, "Patton stormed into an ordnance depot and told the commander that he wanted two thirds of all the stock in the depot. It was in the early days of the depot organization and there wasn't a great deal of stock. Patton did not have authority to do this, but because he had a combat mission to perform and he needed supplies during the early days of his drive across France, he used his rank to demand supplies through improper channels. . . ."

And he got them. The Third Army needed the supplies to continue its drive across France, until in September it finally had to stop because of the force-wide supply crisis which took hold at that time, whereupon the aforementioned Red Ball Express came to his aid. Later, in his drive to relieve the encircled American armies at the Battle of the Bulge, Patton would continue to requisition and siphon off what his men needed without thinking twice.

If Patton had little respect for logisticians, both SHAEF's and his own, neither did most of his field commanders. This attitude was transmitted downwards to their front-line troops who, often wrongly, tended to look down upon the hard-pressed and often heroic rear-echelon supply troops who did their best to supply, transport, and maintain them.

■ ■ ■ ■ ■

Matters were not helped by Eisenhower's head quartermaster, a strutting, pompous egomaniac by the name of Lieutenant General C. H. Lee. Stephen Ambrose, the popular military historian, pulls no punches in characterizing Lee, calling him "the biggest jerk in ETO [European Theater of Operations]." One of Lee's many logistical *faux pax* took place in September, 1944, when he moved his Service of Supply headquarters to Paris, specifically flouting his commanding officer Eisenhower's well-known view that major headquarters should not be located near the temptations of a major city. "The GIs and their generals were furious," Ambrose writes. "At the height of the [post Normandy] supply crisis, Lee had spent his precious time organizing the move, then used up precious gasoline, all so that his entourage could enjoy the hotels of Paris."

It got worse. With 29,000 SOS troops in Paris, the great majority of them involved in some way in the flow of supplies from the beaches and posts to the front, and taking into account what attractions Paris had, including wine, jewels, perfumes, and, of course, women, a black market on a grand scale opened up.

"One of the most notorious of these black markets," Joseph Heiser remembers, "operated at the base of the Eiffel Tower. Word quickly got around that civilians were ready to buy anything the GIs would deliver. The Eiffel Tower was a logical site for a black market. It required no knowledge of Paris and its suburbs for an American to point his truck at the tower in the far distance. Unfortunately, this robbery continued for a long time. Paris was really an open city, and in such a fast-moving city, and in such a fast moving war, enough MPs [military police] and civilian authorities were not available to control black markets."

Of course, Ike was furious with Lee for moving SOS to Paris.

Nevertheless, somewhat inexplicably, Eisenhower—who normally had few reservations about relieving incompetents—let Lee remain at his command until the end of the war.

Ambrose also reveals another gross logistical failing that occurred later that year, when, during the Battle of the Bulge, "to the everlasting disgrace of quartermasters and all other rear echelon personnel" Lee and SOS failed to get proper shoeware for the freezing, snowbound U.S. troops hunkered down on the Belgian-German border. This unforgivable snafu—a World War II expression that stands for Situation Normal All Fucked Up—ultimately caused no less than 45,000 troops, the equivalent of three divisions, to be pulled out of the front line when they contracted trench foot.

All this occurred on General Dwight Eisenhower's watch.

Does this make Eisenhower a poor or indifferent logistician? Probably. Does this disprove our working thesis that the great commanders of history were also, by and large, competent or better logisticians? Not necessarily. Indeed, if anything, Eisenhower, a great leader, strategist, and tactician, and, alas, a mediocre logistician is the exception that proves the rule.

It must be recalled, in Eisenhower's defense, that he commanded the largest expeditionary force in history, one comprising the forces of both the United States, Great Britain, and other nations, on an operation—the invasion of Europe—of unprecedented scale and complexity.

Also he won.

Van Creveld offers his final judgment of the SHAEF logisticians, and, by inference, their commander Ike, thusly: "That the

SHAEF logisticians were not cast in the heroic mold it seems impossible to deny. Yet it is hardly for us, who have seen so many great campaigns come to grief owing to a lack of logistic support, to condemn one which did after all terminate in an undisputed— if possibly belated—success."

Meanwhile, as Heiser reminds us in his memoirs, bravery was not only to be found on the front lines, but amongst the rear echelon troops as well, particularly amongst the ammunition handlers who had to work with cases of high explosives on a daily basis and who frequently were called upon to fight fires among their stores. It is difficult to think of a more dangerous duty than having to wade into a raging, high-explosive ammunition fire, yet many valiant logistics troops did just that. Heiser recalls at least a dozen instances when live ammunition had to be moved out of a fire. "Many times such actions made it possible to win the battle," he rightly points out. The forgotten men who fought these fires, and were consequently seriously wounded or killed, were no less heroes than their brave comrades who stormed ashore on June 6, 1944, or who risked their lives on the front lines in both the European and Pacific theaters of the far flung, global conflict.

■■■■■

By January, 1945, the sheer mass of war material of all kinds issuing forth from the galvanized arsenal of democracy tended to cancel out Eisenhower's apparent neglect of the logistical side, and the gross incompetence of his chief quartermaster Lee. There no longer seemed to be a pressing need to be economical with resources when there was so much sheer *stuff* coming over the Atlantic, now that the Battle of the Atlantic, too, had been won—even if much of it continued to be misshipped, or, even worse, stolen or hoarded.

The stark contrast between the quantity and quality of the bristling Allied arsenal, and the depleted Axis one, became evident following the successful reduction of the Bulge, as the American juggernaut closed in on Hitler's defensive perimeter itself, as Stephen Ambrose notes in *Citizen Soldier*, his authoritative book on the war in Europe. "Even though the battle was raging on Germany's border and German shells had to travel a few kilometers to get there," the historian writes, "such was American productivity that many more American than German shells were arriving. The German attempt to cut Allied lines with their submarines had failed; the Allied attempt to cut supply lines with their Jabos [fighter-bombers] had great success."

"So, the Americans banged away, confident that more shells were on the way." By contrast, "the Germans husbanded their shells, uncertain if any more would arrive."

"This," writes Ambrose, giving credit where credit was due, "was a triumph of American industry and of the American way of war."

As far as ETO's self-regarding Army logisticians were concerned, this, likewise, was also a triumph for *their* philosophy of war, so to speak. Mass logistics, they called it.

Two decades later, when Army logisticians like Joe Heiser were tearing their hair out over what to do with the sheer mass of materiel piled up in Army supply depots and ports in South Vietnam, the drawbacks of this wasteful and incompetent philosophy became evident, causing a national scandal. It can also be argued that the philosophy of mass logistics—essentially, that if you throw enough stuff at a problem it will get solved—slipped over into the civilian sector, helping to explain the disastrous logistics of many American manufacturing firms after the war, which, in many cases, were actually run by former ETO logisticians.

But, in the ETO, mass worked fine. It certainly impressed the overwhelmed German, as one former Wehrmacht soldier, watching the endless river of American men and materiel roll on before him from his hiding place near the Rhine, recalled. "When I saw everything that was going past [me], all the artillery, tanks, and trucks, well, I've got to say, I just flipped. I thought *how can you declare war on such a country?!*"

Indeed.

Or, as the great World War II correspondent, Ernie Pyle, and one of the few correspondents to cover both the European and Pacific theaters of the war in depth, eloquently put it: "In the emergency of war our nation's powers are unbelievable."

"I have heard soldiers say a thousand times, 'If only we could have created all this [materiel] for something good.'" But as Pyle noted, shortly before his own death from a Japanese sniper's bullet in May, 1945, "We rise above our normal powers only in times of destruction." Just as we rose above our normal powers during that previous time of supreme destruction, the Civil War.

And, in the wake of September 11, we are rising above our normal powers again. Hell hath no fury like an America aroused.

■ ■ ■ ■ ■

Perhaps not so surprisingly, it was the vastly undersupplied Far Eastern theater of the war that produced perhaps the war's most logistically astute field commander, Field Marshal Viscount Slim, commander of the storied British Fourteenth Army. The Forgotten Fourteenth it was called at the time, because their supreme commanders in London and Washington, as well as the general public, had supposedly forgotten about them. Slim was a hero of the extraordinary—if now, still, nearly forgotten—Burma campaign against the Japanese.

Slim first became versed in the art of running a shoestring war, as he put it, when, in 1942, he and his underequipped forces were given the task of retaking Syria, which had fallen under the control of the Vichy French. Slim and his crack quartermaster, Alf Snelling, made light of the woefully inadequate equipment available for Slim's operation by calling their ragtag operation

Deficient. And deficient it was. In order to protect his columns as they advanced into Syria from Palestine against the considerable strength of the Vichy Air Force, Slim had but one squadron consisting of only eight planes—four ancient Gladiators, as well as four more up-to-date Hurricanes. The available transport for the drive on Aleppo, the penultimate object of the campaign, was, likewise, pretty skimpy.

This is where Snelling, Slim's ingenious Q-man (as the Brits used to call its quartermaster) shined—or began to. "Snelling's great faculty," notes Ronald Lewin in his biography *Slim: The Standard Bearer*, "was conjuring—producing rabbits out of his hat, making bricks without straw."

He also produced transport where there was none. Thus, notes Lewin, "by stripping the Iraqi command of every available vehicle, including civilian trucks from Baghdad, native boats in the Euphrates, plus a company of donkeys he [Snelling] and Slim were able to cobble together an essential minimum to succeed at the main task."

Thus, too, Slim and his adroit Q-man were well prepared for the yet more formidable logistical difficulties that faced them when they and their men had to make war in the trackless, tropical jungles and swamps of Burma. In Burma Slim fought the Japanese for three years, and he was once again saddled with grossly inadequate supplies—as well as a succession of thick-headed superiors.

It was here where Slim truly distinguished himself, first as a great defensive general, during the initial retreat from Burma in 1942 when he managed to successfully extricate his battered and beleaguered forces 900 miles into India, all the while religiously husbanding his supplies and superintending the morale and health of the men. Later, as an offensive leader in 1944, he marshaled his lean, revitalized forces back into the jungle, outgeneraled and outfought the Japanese at Imphal and Kuhima, and, ultimately retook the former colonial cities of Mandalay and Rangoon.

As Lewin notes, Slim—or "Uncle Bill" as he came to be affectionately known to his troops—was a believer in Socrates's prudent dictum that first "the general must know how to get his men their rations and every other kind of stores needed for war"—especially medicine. In the fetid swamps, rivers, and jungles of Burma, disease posed as formidable an enemy as the Japanese.

"Manpower and other resources might be short," notes Duncan Anderson, another one of Slim's biographers, in a telling passage about Slim's medical—and logistical—side, "but Slim remained inflexible in his insistence on adequate medical supplies, viewing physical health as the key to morale and success. Although his troops shunned antimalarial drugs with the common suspicion that they could cause impotence, Slim ruthlessly enforced their administration.

" 'God helps those who help themselves,' became his and their motto," writes Anderson in his seminal essay about Slim and the Fourteenth in *Churchill's Generals*. Once again, battlefield necessity became the mother of invention, and with Slim and Snelling as the midwives, there were some extraordinary inventions indeed.

"Jute was transformed into parachutes; 'bithness'—strips of locally manufactured and bitumized hessian, became their effective substitute for an all-weather road service. And later the banks of the Chindwin were transformed into an ad hoc boatyard for the construction of a sizeable flotilla of wooden barges and gunboats."

"Few good fighting commanders evoke the same praise from their quartermasters and engineers as they do from their front line soldiers," writes Lewin. "Snelling was amongst his [Slim's] most ardent admirers." (Of course, in the jungle, as Slim, the jungle fighter knew, *everyone* was in the front line; in the Fourteenth Army *everyone* learned how to fight, and well, including office workers, clerks, and babus. This paid off early in 1944 during the

Arakan campaign, when the Japanese targeted the British headquarters at Sinzweya, the so-called administrative box, and were
handily beaten off.)

Slim was that rarity: a fighting commander who could *think*
logistically.

Of course, in the neglected Middle East and Southeast Asian
theaters, where the laws of minimal—not mass—logistics, held
sway, he had to.

Not for nothing that he and his headquarters men dubbed
their last, brilliant offensive—*extended capital*.

It was the thorough planning and logistics behind *extended
capital* that wound up achieving the defeat of the Japanese in
Burma, a signal achievement. That victory later led Slim's some-
time superior, Field Marshal Archibald Wavell, to declare, in his
1953 book *Soldiers and Soldiering*, "the more I study and learn of
war, the more persuaded I am of the importance of administration, or what the Americans call logistics."

Chapter 4

The Soldier
As Customer

"Good logistics is combat power."
—Lieutenant General William "Gus"
Pagonis, Ret., in *Moving Mountains*, 1992

Like most of their comrades in the other branches of the uniformed services, most of the logistics officers who served with the United States Army during World War II returned to civilian life after the end of hostilities in 1945, where they found that their expertise in moving materiel was just as prized, if not more so, by U.S. industry, as it had been by the Pentagon.

One of the brighter members of the minority who didn't depart for the private sector, and instead wound up rising to the top of the logistical profession, while bearing witness to and playing a significant role in the logistics of America's next two overseas wars, was our old friend and former SHAEF planner, Captain Joseph Heiser.

Returning to Washington after the war, Heiser worked on a number of staff assignments following the armistice. By 1950, the able planner had been promoted to lieutenant colonel. Then the Korean War broke out, and Heiser went into action again, this time as ordnance officer for the Army's Seventh Division, where, as he recalls in his memoirs, *Supplying Soldiers*, he and his men were closely involved in the fighting that raged on both sides of the 38th parallel between the U.S. and other United Nations forces, and the North Korean aggressors and their Chinese allies.

Interestingly, Heiser recalls that there was less resentment between rear and front line troops there, partly because the rear and front lines tended to be closer together than in World War II.

Nevertheless, as he writes, there were still many logistical snafus as well as downright stupidity, as he could see when he assumed his posting.

To give one example of the frustration he encountered, he describes one perplexed soldier "who had just arrived after the eighteen hour drive from one of the division's combat units. He had come to get some badly needed antifreeze, only to be told by an implacable supply sergeant that his requisition form was improperly filled out. The stupidity of it all infuriated me."

" 'Do you know what you're doing?' I asked the clerk. 'From now on the rules in these units can be boiled down to one: *we are in business to support the soldier; supporting the units of the Seventh Division is our only business* [my italics].' "

Heiser understood one of the key principles of effective military *and* business logistics, which we will explore in more depth in the next section: *he knew his customer*—in this case, the combat troops of the Seventh Division.

In this respect, he represents a key crossover figure in the history and development of modern logistics, or supply chain management, as the field is now called, because he was one of the first military logisticians to conceive of his mission *in service terms*.

To Heiser, serving his customers meant being as close to them as possible. He writes that at one point of the war "our unit was almost 180 miles from the fighting units that we were supposed to support, I knew we had to move." Thus, when the divisional commander, General Claude Firenbaugh, who was still under the impression that Heiser's ordnance unit was far from the front, ordered Heiser closer to the front lines, his chief ordnance officer—Heiser—could blithely report: "Sir, the ordnance unit is now five miles ahead of your CP [command post]."

"That's what we need here," the general replied. "If all of you move out like Heiser has," Firenbaugh told his staff, "we will make a name for this division."

And so the division, and Heiser's unit, the 707th Ordnance Unit, did.

Despite the less than happy outcome of the Korean War, which resulted in both sides ultimately returning to essentially the same lines they held before the Communist invasion, Heiser was unabashedly proud of his service there. "I must tell you that particular moment [when his commander singled him out with his unit for special praise] began a great time for the 707th Ordnance. With the full commitment of the men, we provided probably the best ordnance support that was ever given to a combat unit."

With Firenbaugh's blessing, Heiser devised many initiatives to further his mission, that is, to keep the customers (i.e., the troops of the Seventh Division) supplied with the ammunition they needed *when they needed it*. To help ensure this, in an inspired move, Heiser attached logistical contact teams, or troubleshooters, to each forward combat unit. As he explains, "These teams maintained equipment and arranged for the distribution of supplies to the combat unit, relieving the fighters of the time-consuming chore of going back to the rear for supplies."

These teams also kept Heiser as up to date as possible *on what was happening within the supply chain he was responsible for*. The veteran logistician's cumulative experience impressed upon him another of the key principles of managing any supply chain: *knowledge is power*.

Forty years later, Heiser's logistical descendant, Gus Pagonis, apparently independently, devised a similar expedient for accomplishing his mission as head U.S. logistician during the Gulf War. *Ghostbusters* he called these logistical spotters, after the popular 1984 film of the same name. Why? Because their job, essentially, was to report on what was there or what wasn't there, that is, disappearing or ghost supplies.

The less flamboyant Heiser didn't have a flashy name for his logistical ombudsmen; however, they performed essentially the same function.

Recently, I interviewed Pagonis. In his book, *Moving Mountains*, he claims that the idea behind having Ghostbusters was his; he claims innocence of the clear Heiser precedent.

I believe him.

As both men's experiences show, when a clear-sighted, flexible, and resourceful logistician like Heiser or Pagonis is in command, military necessity—that is the necessity of keeping the troops in the field happy and well-supplied, and the concomitant necessity of knowing how happy and well-supplied they are at all times—can lead to the same solution, namely, mobile logistical reporting teams, or Ghostbusters.

I have little doubt that if radio and walkie-talkies existed during the early nineteenth century that the Duke of Wellington, with his aforementioned concern about the movement of biscuits, or his equally adroit quartermaster, Archibald Murray, might well have used their own form of Ghostbusters.

■ ■ ■ ■ ■

In his memoirs, Heiser is, perhaps understandably, less nostalgic about the time he spent fifteen years later as the Army's senior logistician in Vietnam. Thanks to poor or nonexistent control, as well as the low priority assigned to and attitude toward logistics and logisticians—one of the many unfortunate earmarks of the generalship of the then outgoing commanding general, General William Westmoreland—the logistical situation in Southeast Asia was a mess, to put it kindly, when Heiser arrived, shortly after the Tet Offensive of January, 1968, to take charge of the Army's 1st Logistics Command. His mission: to straighten that mess out. Otherwise, Heiser, who by then had been promoted to major general, was warned by a friendly fellow general, the low repute in which his fellow logisticians was held was such that he stood a chance of being the last major senior logistician in the U.S. Army.

Things got off badly when, at their first meeting, Heiser's immediate superior, Lieutenant General Frank Mildren, the deputy U.S. Army commander, let him know that he had little faith in logisticians "and that his choice for the job was not Joe Heiser but a combat officer because the logistics mess didn't require logistical knowledge, just a dynamic Army commander to get his job done."

Annoyed but undeterred, Heiser energetically applied himself to his Sisyphean challenge, including the seemingly insurmountable task of trying to sort out the mammoth pile-ups of supplies at the monstrous Cam Ranh and Long Binh supply depots, which by then had become a well-publicized symbol of the mismanaged, increasingly unpopular war. The first thing the new senior logistician did was to change the wrong-headed motto of his command itself, "First with the most." That motto supposedly derived from the great Confederate cavalry general Nathaniel Bedford Forrest's motto, "Firstest with the Mostest"—except that Forrest meant most *men, not most supplies.*

The men at First Log, as Heiser's command was called, who were obviously devotees of the old and long-disproven Army philosophy of mass logistics, had obviously gotten it wrong. "Here I was," Heiser recalls, still livid at the memory, "in the midst of mountains of stuff—almost two million tons—of which we could only identify a third, talking in terms of more and mostest. I said, in my first staff meeting, the first guy who uses that motto from now on will be court-martialed." The First Log's motto was subsequently changed to "First."

Unfortunately, in the hostile intraservice environment in which he operated—as typified by his short-sighted superior general—Heiser could do little about the many large, fixed, logistical bases, or "firebases" as they were called, which had become nests of waste and complacency. These went against everything he had learned in Korea about the need for fast and flexible support of combat units.

In the meantime, the Communist enemy had cunningly shifted a great deal of its offensive to the destruction of U.S. and Allied logistic support capability. The Tet Offensive, though a psychological success, had actually been a costly tactical failure for the Viet Cong, virtually eliminating it as a force to be reckoned with in the South. Heiser is coldly objective about the success of this counter-logistic strategy. "This was an appropriate tactic because our logistics capability in Vietnam was stretched over a 10,000- to 15,000-mile supply route," he reflects.

As a result, Heiser's men not only had to provide supplies to the combat forces, but also had to defend stores and facilities, turning Heiser into a de facto combat commander. "Combat operations in defense of logistics support became a major part of logistics," Heiser notes.

In the end, partly through increased use of computers and business management concepts like Inventory in Motion, Heiser was able to at least partly unravel the logistics mess in Vietnam so that the weight of the American industrial arsenal was more effectively applied.

His efforts were eased somewhat by a welcome development back in Washington: the belated but wise decision to centralize procurement and supply operations for the Army, Navy, and Air Force in one agency, the Defense Logistics Agency.

Not that it mattered much. In the end, the best logistics in the world could not make up for the enemy's superior commitment or the declining public support for the war back home. In an asymmetrical war like the Vietnam conflict—especially one that the American public did not whole-heartedly support—logistics, and logisticians like Heiser, however efficient, wound up being, essentially, meaningless.

■■■■■

The U.S. Army high command entered its next major overseas conflict, the 1991 Gulf War, determined not to repeat the mistakes it had made in Vietnam, including its botched logistics.

First, as Gus Pagonis recalls in his revealing memoir, *Moving Mountains: Lessons in Leadership from the Gulf War*, as well as in his recent interviews with me, the Army brass, still carrying painful memories of the dismaying and disorienting domestic opposition it faced during Vietnam, was firmly resolved never again to get involved in a major overseas war without a solid base of public support. To help ensure this base, Pagonis recalls, in 1971 General Creighton Abrams, the Army chief of staff and former Southeast Asia theater commander, devised a plan, known as the Total Force Concept. Amongst other things, it stipulated that in the future most berths in the Army's combat and infantry units would be filled by regular, active-duty soldiers, whereas slots for all logistics personnel—transport personnel, water purification personnel, forklift operators, and so forth— would be filled by reservists.

"The logic," says Pagonis, himself a veteran of the Vietnam quagmire and heartbreak, "was sound: if a war can't be fought without support personnel, and if most support personnel are in the reserve ranks, then the Army can't be asked to fight much of a war unless the politicians are willing to let the reserves get called up. That precisely is what happened in the Gulf War. Almost every single person in the United States was touched personally by the Gulf War—either a relative, or a friend, or a neighbor was called to service."

Thus, through Abram's Total Force Concept, the United States Army entered the Gulf War with a full *moral* arsenal of public support, to complement its sizable materiel one. We recently saw the same concept activated at the start of the Afghanistan war, when reserves were once again called up.

Another priority for the Pentagon following the Vietnam debacle was to clean up its logistical support act. The Army could not afford another massive, snafu-laden depot like the ones at Normandy and Cam Ranh Bay, where, as Pagonis writes, "it was impossible to determine which supplies were on hand or where they could be found." Neither could it afford the dreadful, immobile firebases of Vietnam—"those stupid firebases," as Pagonis still refers to them, "which," as he told me, "became permanent fixtures in the middle of the jungle and made soldiers very complacent, because they knew they would always come back in three days to the warmth and luxuries of the firebase."

One of the first things Pagonis discussed with his boss, Norman Schwarzkopf, upon being appointed deputy commanding general for logistics for Desert Shield, the initial build-up phase of the Gulf War, was the need to make logistical bases in the current operation mobile ones—an idea he took from his ancestor, Alexander the Great.

Schwarzkopf readily agreed because his own frustrating experience as an assistant division commander in Vietnam had impressed him with the importance of getting logistics right.

Schwarzkopf, whose close relationship with his chief quartermaster resembled the ones Wellington and Slim enjoyed with their quartermasters, Murray and Snelling, respectively, had already made perhaps his most significant logistical decision at the start of the operation in asking for Pagonis to be his chief logistician. A highly decorated Vietnam veteran, Pagonis boasted both extensive field and headquarters experience, including combat experience, as well as a graduate degree in business management from Pennsylvania State University. At Penn State, Pagonis had become versed in the "integrated logistics" approach to business logistics, as it was then called (more about that in the next chapter). Pagonis's varied background would steer him well in his new assignment.

He certainly had to fill a large berth. As deputy commanding general for logistics and commander of the Army Central Support Command, Pagonis was responsible for all matters relating to fuel, water, food, vehicles, ammunition, and all classes of supply, as well as, in a crucial addition to his duties which he himself had demanded, port and airport control; Pagonis knew from his previous battlefield experience, as well as from his business logistics training at Penn State, that it was vital for him to have control of *as much of the supply chain as possible.*

In addition, Pagonis was also in charge of obtaining and securing the cooperation of the host nation, Saudi Arabia. Few quartermasters or logisticians have ever been asked to shoulder such an enormously complicated and politically demanding task, or group of tasks, or had as many men serving directly under him. "At the peak of Desert Shield," Norman Schwarzkopf recalls in his own memoirs, "he [Pagonis] had nearly ninety-four different Reserve and National Guard units under his command. Somehow he managed to integrate them all into his system."

Pagonis was an inspired administrator as well as a born diplomat. The latter skill was especially handy in his role as host nation coordinator, as his admiring chief recalls: "The Saudis had promised to help with fuel, water, and transportation but hadn't fully appreciated what they were in for; nor had any arrangements been made for accommodations," Schwarzkopf writes. "With tens of thousands of Americans streaming in, both we and our hosts were at a loss where to put them until Pagonis discovered that the kingdom had huge numbers of tents in storage—for the annual pilgrimage to Mecca. . . . The *hajj* wasn't until late spring or early summer, so Pagonis was able to acquire the tents and create villages for the troops."

"For the central briefing areas," Schwarzkopf wrote, describing Pagonis's ingenious solution, "there would eventually be huge *fest* tents shipped from Germany, where they'd been used for beer festivals, another Pagonis inspiration."

Not everything about Desert Shield, the build-up phase of the war and the one that Pagonis essentially dominated, was improvised. In fact, he was working from a simple and flexible plan that he had devised upon first arriving at his desert command. Pagonis's logistical plan divided the aspects of the American deployment in the Gulf into three phases: first, *reception* of troops in the theater; second, *forward movement*, when the troops in theater actually went into battle, whenever that might be—and it is important to remember that when he and his staff arrived in Saudi Arabia in August, 1990, they had no idea when, if at all, that might be; and lastly, *sustainment* of the troops once in battle. The basic plan could not have been simpler.

Wisely, Schwarzkopf gave his chief logistician the authority to execute his plan. He also saw to it that Pagonis, who had arrived in the theater as a two-star general, received his third star.

"The first thing we discussed [after I arrived] was that we cannot have a mess like Vietnam," Pagonis told me. "There needed to be a single [three-star level] point of [logistical] contact."

"By controlling and knowing what was on the ships, and by also making sure I had the authority of the United States of what to ship and when to ship it, it made a world of difference," he says.

Pagonis used his knowledge and control—as well as his new rank—to establish a logistical regime, or empire, really, which looked at once to the past and to the future for its operating methodology and philosophy.

One of the most important Pagonis innovations, as noted, was the mobile logbase. If and when the call to do battle with Saddam was issued, Pagonis decided that the coalition troops' logistical bases would have to move with them. "Our willingness to place these bases alongside (and, in some cases, in front of) the combat arms troops was surprising to some," he writes, "but I would argue that it didn't contradict established doctrine. Instead we tailored doctrine to the needs of the theater. We [also] restricted the logbases to the smallest number of absolutely indispensable items—food, fuel, water, and ammo—mainly to ensure that they'd be movable as the front line advanced."

Another key Pagonis innovation during Desert Shield—which lasted from August, 1990 to January, 1991, when the call to arms was finally issued and the air war component of Desert Storm began—was the logistical cell, or log cell, an ad hoc think tank comprising a squad of his top logisticians who created and practiced different possible logistical scenarios—or what-if scenarios as I call them—in anticipation of the real thing. This deviated even further from Army doctrine, as Pagonis readily admits.

"It made sense to me to separate out the long range planning functions from the logistical operations that support combat on a day-to-day basis—and also to make sure that the former stayed closely tuned in to the latter's activities," Pagonis says. He did not want another SHAEF-like brontosaurus. The logistics command—or log cell—was lean and mean, never comprising more than a few dozen planners.

Clearly, like his predecessor, Joe Heiser, Pagonis also understood that knowledge was power, that the more knowledge he had of the operation the better he would be able to manage, and the better he would be able to serve his customers or troops.

Hence, the need for his Ghostbusters, his "eyes, ears, and nose," as he put it, who traveled to every corner of his empire, as he jestingly called it, and reported logistical problems and dilemmas back to him, which he would try to solve on the spot. If such problems were systemic, he would refer those problems to the log cell to unscramble.

Meanwhile, too, Pagonis showed that, when it came to requisitioning supplies and men, he could, if necessary, be a Patton, too, plundering military outfits as they came in to solve his personnel needs—with his boss's approval, of course. "If a stevedore unit showed up when he didn't need any more stevedores," his commander smilingly recalls, "he'd say 'I hereby christen thee a transportation outfit. You guys go out and drive trucks.' The reservists would grumble, 'I didn't come over to drive a truck.' But Pagonis's attitude was, 'We'll talk about that when the war is over. Right now we don't have time.'"

Finally, on December 29, 1990, with Saddam still adamant in his refusal to obey the United Nations Security Council's resolution that he withdraw from Kuwait, Schwarzkopf convened his war council at Riyahd. At that council he discussed his plan to pull an "end run" around the Iraqi Army, a strategy built around the ambitious, if essentially simple, logistical plan that Pagonis and his people at the log cell had created.

"Does everyone agree that Pagonis's plan can work?" Schwarzkopf asked, according to Pagonis's recollection of that dramatic moment. "At that point, still standing at the front of the room with a pointer in my hand, I interjected, 'Sir, this logistical plan can happen, and we will make it happen.'"

At his commander's request, he then signed his briefing chart, including maps, twenty-one-day timetable, corps and logistics movement, and wrote along the bottom, "Logisticians will not let you or your soldiers down. William Pagonis, 29 December 1990."

And, as history records, they didn't.

■■■■■

To be sure, one of the more interesting and instructive aspects of Pagonis's philosophy, and one that is relevant to this book, is that, like Heiser, he envisioned and conceived his function as a businessman would. "We were a service business," he says, "the troops were our customers, and we had to win and retain their loyalty."

That explains one of the best-loved and remembered Pagonis innovations from the Gulf War: the Wolfmobile, mobile canteen-like trailer trucks that brought stateside-style fast-food service, complete with all the amenities, to forward troops in the desert. As he recalls, "Who says we can't get hamburgers and hot dogs out to the troops?" And so he and his men did. Eventually, with the aid of his Saudi hosts, he was able to put 1,200 Wolfmobiles into the field. Like other great logisticians, Pagonis—along with his commander, Norman Schwarzkopf—understood that a happy army was an efficient and combat-ready army. And those Wolfmobiles went a long way towards making that army happy.

To Pagonis, the principles of sound military and sound business logistics were, and are, essentially the same. The main difference was that the bottom-line was different. "What's the biggest difference between logistics in the military and in the private sector?" he wrote in 1992. "Without doubt, it's our respective bottom lines, and how we think about them. The military focuses on life and death, whereas business measures profit."

However, Pagonis writes, the differences between the two were "more of a matter of degree than of kind." The basic principles of military logistics—foresight, flexibility, economy, simplicity, cooperation, innovation—are also the criteria by which his counterparts in the civilian sector ought to be judged.

With Pagonis's can-do attitude as well as his can-do track record, it was little wonder that Sears, Roebuck, which has a history of being logistically aware (as we shall further see in the following chapter), asked Pagonis to prove his thesis by taking charge of its logistics. Nor was it any wonder that Pagonis readily exchanged his military cap for a civilian one and accepted the post as Sears' vice president in charge of logistics.

■ ■ ■ ■ ■

Not so surprisingly, Pagonis, the exemplary military logistician turned ultimate business logistician, is still in the job. Today, Pagonis still uses Ghostbusters at Sears; he even calls them that, too.

Significantly, in 1997, the U.S. Marines thought highly enough of the Pagonis-Sears operation—as well as of the strategic importance of logistics—to assign one of its most promising combat commanders to train with Pagonis for two years.

Evidently the Marines were pleased with the result. When the 26th Marine Expeditionary Unit was sent to Afghanistan in November 2001, its commander was Pagonis's proud former student, Colonel Andrew Frick. Meanwhile, in another illustration of the increasing convergence of and interchangeability of military and business logistics, and one that helped catalyze my own logistical thinking process, as part of the logistics revolution of the 1990s I worked with the Air Force, helping to upgrade its information infrastructure.

If you recall from the Prologue, my last three steps en route to discovering the Tri-Level View brought me near the end of my logistical Burma Road: first, that any company's, or service branch's, delivery system could best be envisioned as a black box.

This black box had then morphed into a plumbing system, with valves like those of a kitchen sink. Upon further investigation and reflection, I had also come to see that this plumbing system could *also* be visualized as an electronic circuit board, with five "voltages" that could be measured at the front of the black box, the back of the black box, or anywhere inside of it: cost, time, location, configuration, and characteristics.

In the meantime, I also worked with Ryder, the trucking firm, which was in the process of transforming itself into a third-party logistics provider, that is, a company that created and provided logistics solutions for other firms (more about that development in Chapter 6), bringing state-of-the-art facilities and transportation, business processes, and software to firms like OfficeMax, a nationwide office supply retailer, and Procter & Gamble, a consumer goods manufacturer.

As a result of *that* experience I *also* realized that a delivery system could *also* be represented as a three layer pie. The pie could be broken down into three layers: physical infrastructure, services infrastructure, information infrastructure. Further, I saw that each layer could be cut into four quarters: customer service, transportation, warehousing, and finance. Twelve pieces altogether: big pie. Juicy pie.

Peering further into my black box turned plumbing system, turned circuit board, turned pie I realized that companies had a choice of either managing, or trying to manage, all dozen pieces on their own, or they could give them to third party logistics providers like Ryder.

The crystal ball became clearer.

Meanwhile, at about this time the Air Force decided to use a bit of civilian third-party logistics expertise to clean up *its* logistics mess, especially its tangled information infrastructure. My brief on the Air Force job was to show the Air Force how it could sharpen its warehousing technology. This led me to wonder: What, after all, *is* a warehouse? In the Air Force, several pallets bolted together might be rolled from a supply depot onto an aircraft. That aircraft might then fly around the world as, effectively, a flying depot. Those pallets could then be continuously maintained in the air or parachuted out over the Persian Gulf to a makeshift supply depot on the ground. Those pallets might then be damaged when they landed at the desert depot, or even looted—as they indeed were by some of our less scrupulous soldiers during the Gulf War. (Yes, there was hoarding and looting during Desert Storm, too, but not nearly to the same degree that occurred during World War II.)

In any case, it was absolutely vital for the Air Force to have a reliable inventory of those pallets, and one that could be tracked in a master inventory-control system for an entire region. Lives were at risk.

As I pondered the Air Force's snafu-laden extant information technology—which was also causing problems down the line for the Defense Logistics Agency—I got to thinking about what a warehouse *is*. Was a pallet in and of itself a warehouse? Or is it part of one virtual warehouse for the entire Air Force?

That is when it occurred to me: the principles that exist *locally* inside a warehouse are the same as those that exist *globally between* warehouses. What happens to goods within an ordinary warehouse? Answer: They are *transferred* or *buffered*—that is, held in place—*reconfigured*, that is, they are added to other pallets or boxes of goods, without changing the inherent characteristics of themselves or others, or they could be *modified*—opened, depleted, enhanced, or otherwise transformed—into something other than what they inherently were when they arrived at the physical Air Force warehouse.

Then I realized that the same processes—transferring,

buffering, reconfiguring, and modifying—could *also* exist *between* warehouses.

I was getting somewhere.

Of course, I had not had my epiphany-inducing encounter with that sugar packet yet. Before we get there, and now that I have inculcated you in both the glorious and inglorious history of military logistics, let us backtrack a bit—say, to the eighteenth century—and take a look at the glorious and inglorious (mostly the latter) history and development of business logistics.

Chapter 5

Early Business Logistics: The South Sea Bubble and the Shipping Room Mob

"There is nothing more requisite in business than dispatch."
> **—Joseph Addison, quoted in _The Drummer_, 1716**

In 1962 management expert Peter Drucker published a landmark article about business logistics, or distribution as it was then called, in _Fortune_ magazine. "Distribution" he said flatly— after pointing out that almost fifty cents of every dollar the U.S. customer spends goes for activities _after_ the goods are made—"is one of the sadly neglected, most promising areas of American business."

"We know little more about distribution," Drucker declared, "than Napoleon's contemporaries did about the interior of Africa. We know it is there, and we know it is big; and that's about all."

By the time I became involved with distribution, or supply chain management as the field had come to be called, we had not learned much more about this sadly neglected, if promising area, despite some very considerable advances in logistical thought.

Somewhere along the line there had been a disconnect between theory and practice. Indeed, by giving precedence to a rather blinkered view of the marketing process that focused on sales and scanted supply concerns, American business had actually taken a giant step *backwards*.

Put another way, American business had forgotten who the customer was. Something was wrong with this picture. But why? How?

To answer that question I turned to the extant literature on the history of logistics, of which there is a considerable amount, mostly written by academics. Unfortunately, most of it is deadly.

This is a great shame, since the story of the development and growth of American business logistics—including the history and development of logistical thought—when turned to one side, so to speak, is the story of American business itself including how American business has perceived itself, with the numerous changes in the role assigned to business logistics—or physical distribution, as it was called until recently—and the ever-changing definition of the functions associated with it, forming a convenient prism through which to view the history of the American economy itself.

Also, as is the case with its twin story of the history of military logistics, the story and history of business logistics has its heroes and dunces, its shiny victories and its spectacular failures.

Who said that logistics was boring?

In fact, as we will see, one of the greatest obstacles that the logistical profession has faced, and continues to face, *is* the erroneous perception that distribution and supply concerns *are* boring, or unimportant. As we shall see, nothing could be further from the truth.

But we are getting ahead of ourselves.

Perhaps the best place to begin our selective history of business logistics and logistical thought is with the tale of one of the first, and arguably, the most spectacular business failure in modern history: the South Sea Bubble.

The South Sea Bubble—which, like many "bubbles," including the recent much-discussed dot.com bubble, was attributable to a combination of logistical ignorance, hubris, and downright fraud—is the name history has given to the apocalyptic failure of the world's first great international trading company and wholesaler, the South Sea Trading Company. Founded by Robert Harley, an enterprising London businessman, the company gained immediate fame when, in 1711, Harley and his partners managed to persuade the British government, then deeply in debt, to give them a monopoly over certain of Britain's lucrative trade routes with South America and the South Sea Islands. In return, the new trading company agreed to assume the bulk of that debt, which then stood at more than £10 million, in addition to an annual payment to the Crown of £600,000.

Thus blessed, the chartered company, and its small fleet of ships, became the leading provisioner to England of the diverse South Sea spices, South American fruit and tobacco, and all sorts of other exotic—and expensive—stuff. In this way, it also became, one could say, the world's first brand name. The hype surrounding the South Sea Trading Company grew even bigger in 1718 when the sovereign himself, King George I, became its governor, creating yet new confidence in the enterprise, which yielded its initial investors massive returns reminiscent of the heady early days of the dot.com bubble.

The American colonists fell under the company's magic spell

just as readily as did their fellow subjects back home in England. The South Sea Company *was* the company. If you were a Boston or New York merchant and placed an order with it, you could rely on it delivering the goods on time, give or take a week or two, allowing for the moods of the seas. Somewhere in the middle of the growing bubble of misinformation and hype around the company, there *was*, in fact, a company.

With that sort of reputation, in addition to the very conspicuous sight of the company's original directors reveling in their newfound lucre, other investors soon became interested in getting in on what seemed like a sure thing. In 1719, eight years after the company was chartered, they got their chance when His Majesty's government approved a further agreement under which the government's creditors could exchange their claims on the Crown in return for stock in the by now famous firm. A swarm of such creditors rushed to buy stock. They were joined by a large number of ordinary citizens in Britain and the American colonies who also decided to invest, thereby pushing the value of South Sea stock from £128.5 to £1,000 in a matter of months. The gold rush was on.

Unfortunately, it was a fool's gold rush, for these hapless investors were, by now, largely banking on a phantom. Unbeknownst to the public, as a result of a combination of bad seas, poor communications, and a generous helping of mismanagement and malfeasance, the company's once relatively reliable system for the purchase and delivery of its cornucopia of goods had utterly broken down. By the time anyone realized the extent of the logistical bad information bubble, which had now fed into the speculative bad information bubble, it was too late to do anything about it. Meanwhile, Harley and his friends took a powder.

Of course, if the S.S.T.C. had had a few modern-day troubleshooters or Ghostbusters in its employ, and the British government, which had chartered the company, had had a proper stock control apparatus, the ensuing South Sea Bubble, as it became known, could have been avoided. A telegraph system might also have helped. But this was still the early eighteenth century. Telegraph would not arrive until the nineteenth. Buyers and suppliers on both sides of the Atlantic, blithely unaware of the logistical rot at the heart of the company, as well as the increasing corruption surrounding it, continued to place their orders with the company, and purchased stock in it. And so the bubble grew and grew.

The fledgling London press, then at the start of its scandal-mongering days, eagerly rushed into the information breach, and reported the true state of the company's affairs. Although some of the company's original investors, as well as a number of corrupt government ministers, managed to enrich themselves, most wound up losing their investments. Many were left in ruins; some committed suicide. In the wake of the burst bubble, the House of Commons was forced to convene an official court of inquiry into the sordid affair. Its scathing report, issued in 1721, attributed the fiasco to a combination of greed, gullibility—and bad information. The South Sea Company itself, which continued to sail the seas until the mid-nineteenth century, was allowed to retain its charter, but only after completely revising its way of operating—including its logistical reporting procedures. However, the system, as well as the idea, of having chartered companies had been gravely weakened. The international business world had had its first great scandal, and logistics was at the heart of it.

Chartered companies' problems aside, America's distribution problem—as the logistical parlance of the day called it—remained a fairly simple one during the eighteenth and most of the nineteenth centuries, while the American economy continued to be agriculturally based. Such manufacturing that existed was concentrated along the Eastern seaboard. With the United States still heavily reliant on imports, especially for finished products, major import-export centers were concentrated in cities with good harbors, including New York, Boston, and Atlanta. The bulk of America's trading and commercial shipping activity involved the movement of agricultural surpluses from the Midwest and South to the East, in exchange for imported or homemade goods, a relatively simple transaction. The latter was facilitated by the construction of America's first, rough (very rough) highways, one of the few items that the parsimonious (and not especially rich) U.S. Congress and various state legislatures agreed were worth spending tax revenue on.

To augment the highways eventually, in 1825, came the epochal Erie Canal, and other kindred civil engineering feats, like the wondrous Brooklyn Bridge, which upon its completion in 1883 became the world's first suspension bridge. Today these landmark projects are considered sight-seeing attractions. Of course, they are, but it is well to remember that their original *raison d'etre* was to expedite the movement of goods and products. Thus, the nation's embryonic transportation system, which we have seen formed the basis of Ulysses Grant's winning logistic-based strategy in the Civil War (see Chapter 2), also helped form the basis of its original economic identity.

The structure and dynamics of America's logistical environment, how the distribution task, hitherto deemed to comprise the simple storage and shipment of goods, was defined and to whom in the booming economy that task devolved upon, changed dramatically after the Civil War when the country shifted to a mass production, railroad-reliant economy.

During Reconstruction the fast-expanding rail network added a new dimension to the logistical picture by linking local markets with new regional and national ones, contributing to potential scale economies in the booming manufacturing sector.

With the potential for savings, firms began to wrest the distribution task back from wholesalers. They wanted to be in charge of supply and shipping.

This turned out to be a mixed blessing; manufacturers, baffled by the new challenge they had taken on, found that their logistical problems were more complex than they had bargained for. The differentiation of products, along with expanding markets, put new strains on the nation's overtaxed land-distribution and transportation system.

The arrival of the internal combustion engine at the end of the nineteenth century, and with it, motorized transport, further complicated the distribution challenge, making it necessary for companies and firms to incorporate logistics into their market strategy, if they were to survive. Businessmen, who previously had regarded distribution as external to their affairs—as something occurring outside their walls—now were forced to see it as intrinsic to it.

Thus, by the outbreak of World War I, there was, in the words of economic historian Bernard LaLonde, an increasing awareness that "a combination of physical distribution with market demand and cost efficiency in the physical movement of goods were key aspects of a firm's struggle to remain competitive."

Quite a transformation in perspective for a mere half century. The very *idea* of distribution had become an active, indeed motorized, one.

With business at the dawn of a brave new scientific era, it fell to the academic sector to translate the new parameters of American business, and to rapidly enlarge the view of the distribution function into managerial theory.

The first theorist to take up the baton, and in some ways still the most important, was Archibald Shaw, a Harvard professor who bravely attempted to set out a body of principles and generalities that he believed to be the preconditions for the shaping of a new science of business, one combining the best of the old Main Street business ethos with the energy and ambition of the fast, new automotive age. He incorporated these thoughts in his 1916 book, *An Approach to Business Problems.*

Although not especially easy to read, *An Approach to Business Problems* was, in many ways, a visionary book; in some ways, it still is. Much of the book, which became the first best-selling business management book, focused on *the place* of the forward-looking, American business in the modern twentieth-century economy. Shaw devoted much of his attention to distribution and its relationship to the emerging marketing philosophy of America. As the prescient Harvard don saw it, marketing consisted of two synergistically linked halves: demand creation—or what is today considered marketing—and demand satisfaction—or physical supply. Or logistics.

Here is how he put it: "The physical distribution of goods is a problem distinct from the creation of demand, though it is one which must be considered at every step in any marketing solution arrived at. Not a few costly failures in distribution campaigns have been due to such a lack of coordination between demand creation and physical supply . . . Instead of being a subsequent problem the question of supply must be met and answered *before* the work of distribution begins . . ."

Put simply, delivering the goods was part and parcel of the process of selling them.

At first blush, this essentially common-sense dictum might not seem revolutionary today. Nevertheless it would take the better part of the rest of the century for American business to get the message.

And there are still many businesses that *don't* get it.

Other academic-based writers in the 1920s took Shaw's functional approach to marketing even further. One, Northwestern

University professor, Fred Clark, likewise saw the exchange functions, as they were called then, as one part of the marketing process, and the physical distribution function as another. Clark was also one of the first to speak of the principle of concentration and dispersion in the movement of goods. He was also especially interested in the role of transportation rates as a factor affecting marketing delineation and competitive success.

"Other things being equal," Clark wrote, "the seller who has the lowest transportation rates on the materials, equipment, and supplies which he uses, and on the shipment of his product to market, can sell at the lowest prices, make the greatest profit, and, if his supply is great enough, even control the market."

Translation: distribution counts.

In 1927, another business management expert by the name of Ralph Borsodi devoted a book to the problem of rising distribution costs. Borsodi observed that "in the 50 years between 1870 and 1920 the cost of distributing necessities and luxuries has nearly trebled, while product costs have gone down by one fifth."

"What we are seeing in production," he concluded, "we are losing in distribution."

Sounding what amounted to a note of apostasy in an age that saw the dawn of mass marketing—including the publication of a best-selling book, *The Greatest Salesman of All Time*, by evangelist Ralph Barton, in which the author described Jesus Christ as a successful salesman—Borsodi laid the blame for ballooning distribution costs on American industry's obsession with sales, which caused it to lose its competitive bearings. "Manufacturers engaged in mass promotion and mass selling have been the active factors in the development of extravagant marketing and unnecessary transportation," he declared. "They are responsible for the breaking down of that skillful and skeptical buying by retailers and consumers which tends to raise standards and to lower costs."

Further, he charged, logistically retarded manufacturers were engaged in pointless, no-holds-barred battles for national markets that were often distant from those in which they could market and distribute their goods most efficiently and economically.

The emerging logistic consciousness was also reflected to some extent in the growing number of business periodicals, such as *Sales Management*, and later, *Fortune*. Thus, in a particularly prescient 1929 article in *Sales Management* by journalist Richard Webster, entitled "Careless Physical Distribution: A Monkey Wrench in Sales Machinery," the author tried to call readers' attention to the essentiality of physical distribution to sales and profits.

Webster ascribed part of the problem to the lack of reliable measurements with which to track the physical flow of goods. Existing cost-accounting procedures, he pointed out, were inadequate, failing to pinpoint the real cost of excessive inventories and customer satisfaction.

Interestingly, too, in a note that would be sounded again and again by other logistic pamphleteers, Webster also attributed many manufacturers' blindness to the distribution dimension to what can only be described as an antilogistic bias based on *image*, that is, the impression that distribution and supply concerns and activities did not require much intelligence and so could be left to dummies. Thus, he complained, despite the manifest and growing importance of distribution activities, such work, both on the planning and applied level was too often relegated to "factory minds," or the "shipping room mob," as Peter Drucker would later call them. But, of course, logistics was not then, and not now, for dummies.

One company that *did* get the distribution message and also saw fit to assign its finest minds to it was Sears, Roebuck. When that quintessentially American company was founded in 1886, there were still only 38 states in the United States, and most of the company's deliveries were made by horse-drawn carriage. Beginning in 1919, the forward-looking retailer, seeing that "the only truly adequate way of examining individual stages [of distribution] was to see the whole," according to Robert Wood, began adopting a holistic view of distribution. General Robert Wood, the company's first head of distribution, the job held later by Gus Pagonis, had been the U.S. Army's chief supply officer during World War I, and had directed the construction of the Panama Canal. In 1928, this hard-charging former military logistician became company president. Wood understood that, as he said, "in making and selling typewriters it made very little sense to run through the plant those parts that are purchased on the outside and sold for replacement . . . and that unless one traces the entire physical flow, one does not see them."

Thus, Sears was, arguably, America's first logistically aware company, a tradition which continues to the present day—including its admirable tradition of having former military logisticians like Wood and Pagonis run the supply side of things.

Henry Ford was another manufacturer who understood the strategic and competitive importance of the distribution function. His successful business philosophy fused the Victorian era's concern with satisfying the customer with the dynamism of the age of mass production to create America's first popular mass-produced motor car, the Model T.

Ford's place in American economic history as the progenitor of the Model T, of course, is well known.

What is less well known is that in his embrace of the concept of physical flow he was also a major logistical innovator. No industrialist better understood the meaning of the extended enterprise, or, for that matter, of customer satisfaction, than he did. In creating his great factory at River Rouge, a temple of mass production if there ever was one, the car builder saw his plant as the end point of an intercontinental supply chain that began with the rubber plants of Southeast Asia, from whence the tires for his phaetons originated, extended through the four walls of the plant itself, and culminated in the Ford customer's garage.

Ford's vision of an intercontinental supply chain, managed and synchronized from company headquarters in Detroit, proved beyond the scope of both the rudimentary accounting and information gathering technology which existed in his day, as well as the isolationist mentality of preglobal Coolidge era America.

Or, as one observer simply put it, "Ford's concept never got off the ground because no one could understand what he was talking about." Another half a century would pass before people at the highest levels of American industry could understand what Henry Ford was talking about when he preached the mantra of "transcontinental materials flow," or would possess the tools, or the mindset, to put talk into practice.

Nevertheless, the 1920s were a sort of golden age of logistic thought, a time when physical distribution, previously seen as essentially a static function comprised principally of storage and transportation, began to take on the aspect of an important corporate function, one that was an intrinsic part of the marketing process and a vital element of the modern American firm's competitive strategy.

This process continued upon the onset of the Great Depression, which also brought a new emphasis on customer satisfaction and encouraged numerous firms to follow Sears, Roebuck and Ford's examples and give distribution, and their distribution personnel, the attention and status they both deserved and needed.

Nevertheless, distribution's nagging image problem, the tendency, as Webster put it, to relegate it to "factory minds," continued to prevent the Shaw/Ford vision of distribution from taking hold.

Although, as we have seen, World War II was essentially a war of logistics, in the most comprehensive sense—that is, it is a struggle between the American arsenal and the Axis one—the war itself actually did little to advance the principles of sound distribution. With the American government now industry's principal customer, the primary criteria for measuring customer satisfaction—cost and reliability—took a back seat to the overarching national-cum-military need for mass and speed.

As we have seen, American industry succeeded in delivering that mass and speed. Mass logistics, the prevailing logistic philosophy, was called. And it worked.

However, not surprisingly, many of the goods produced under its umbrella were, in fact, unreliable and costly. Perhaps the best example of the benefits and drawbacks of this theory was our old friend, Henry J. Kaiser. Rising to the occasion, Kaiser's shipyards turned out a stupendous number of ships in record-breaking time.

Unfortunately, their reliability—their seaworthiness—actually left much to be desired. One of the poorly kept secrets of the war was that the hastily built prefabricated Liberty Ships had a tendency to break apart in extreme weather, a discovery that briefly cast a pall over Kaiser and his remarkable mass production achievement, especially after he was called to testify about the failures before a Senate investigating committee chaired by the Right Honorable Harry S. Truman of Missouri.

But the hubbub died away. As far as Kaiser's chief customer, Uncle Sam, was concerned, Kaiser had delivered the goods. So what if a few of his ships sank? What counted was that most of them didn't.

In short, even though Kaiser was, by dint of the naval arsenal his shipyards and factories produced, and the speed with which they produced them, arguably, the greatest logistic hero of the war, he himself was, at least by civilian standards, not the best lo-gistician (a point that was driven home after the war when Mr. Can Do decided to take on Detroit by manufacturing his own automobile, the Henry J., and lost his shirt).

Distribution began to receive some of its long-denied status in 1948 when the then leading U.S. management association, the American Management Association, formally defined physical distribution management as "the movement and handling of goods from the point of production to the point of consumption."

However, defining distribution didn't necessarily bring dis-tributive clarity.

Joe Heiser, then a colonel, discovered this truth for himself in 1953 when, as he recalls in his memoirs, he and a group of other regular Army logisticians were invited by a consortium of Chicago businessmen to inspect and analyze their own distrib-ution practices and report their observations. In the event, Heiser and his military colleagues were somewhat under-whelmed by what they found. His downbeat conclusion, which was reported in the press, much to his discomfort, was that "the right hand [marketing] didn't know what the left [distrib-ution] was doing." His corporate hosts, who had been expect-ing a top rating from Heiser & Co., were predictably scandalized, but he was right. In most American companies, the marketing department *didn't* know what distribution was doing, nor did the marketers care.

Thus, except for a few farsighted companies that came to see physical distribution as part of their strategic mission, and orga-nized their distribution function and personnel accordingly, dis-tribution continued to be the odd man out of American business well into the 1960s.

A series of articles in the business management press, not dis-similar to the ones published by Webster and his fellow journalistic truth seekers thirty years earlier, once again brought this truth seekers, and self-defeating, state of affairs to the fore.

The first of these, written by Bud Reese, associate editor of *Inventory Management*, appeared in October, 1961. In his article, entitled "Physical Distribution: the Neglected Function," Reese estimated that, for the average firm, physical distribution consumed between twenty-five percent and thirty-three percent of each sales dollar, making it the third highest cost of doing business after labor and materials. Nevertheless, despite the manifest importance of distribution, and the lost sales caused by faulty distribution processes and mediocre distribution personnel, he declared, distribution continued to hover in a kind of corporate twilight zone, neither here nor there. Sound familiar?

To help dramatize his point, Reese sketched out this rather mild, but still disturbing Nightmare of Shipping:

> He read the company's ad and talked to its salesman. He liked what he had read and heard; and placed a trial order, to be delivered in six weeks.
>
> That was seven weeks ago—and still no sign of the shipment. He [the purchasing agent] has decided to wait another three days before canceling *and he has decided to stick with his regular supplier* [Reese's italics]."

Up music. . . .

Funny? Perhaps. Except if you were the salesman who lost that sale and, perhaps, his job and the jobs of others working with him, as a result of his company's failure to deliver the goods.

Part of the problem, according to Reese, was that, in most companies, distribution was poorly organized. "Too many physical distribution functions are left to fall between the chairs, creating many 'grey areas' where objectives, policies, and organizational lines are at best fragmentary, if they exist at all," he opined.

With no one in charge, it was no wonder that most American companies were not able to deliver the right goods in the right time at the right place.

The principal culprit for the hydra-headed problem, according to Reese? Guess who? Those obtuse fellows in marketing.

Well, Reese didn't quite put it that way, but he came close:

"Sales are being lost and advertising claims are falling on deaf ears because of faulty physical distribution," he declared, "and marketing men are primarily to blame for permitting this situation to exist."

According to Reese, it was these same self-important, self-centered marketing men who were also responsible for, and even secretly relished, the distribution man's intrafirm image problem, the notion that somehow distribution was the domain of *untermenschen*.

Thus Reese recounted an illuminating conversation with a contemporary business consultant who recalled that "not infrequently, in discussing job responsibility with senior marketing executives we have had them wryly add, 'Oh yes, another part of my job includes liaison with the plant shipping department.' "

Amazingly, a half century after Shaw's dictate about the independence of and commensurate importance of marketing and distribution, the two functions were as segregated, and the latter as derogated, as ever before.

Not surprisingly, because of American industry's endemic logistic blind spot, Reese was not very optimistic about the future, closing his article with the following dark vision:

In 1965 [four years hence] there will be many physical distribution managers. They will come from traffic and transportation, from warehousing, from industrial engineering, from production, marketing and sales. Each will have greater scope and greater breadth of vision than the present pioneers of distribution management. . . .

I see such a man at his desk. It's a clean desk, except for rows of push-buttons, intercoms and other executive gadgets. Behind him, and on all sides, there are live charts and graphs, pulsating with electronic recordings of up-to-the-moment inventories at all distribution points. . . .

As the distribution manager of 1965 sits in his white tower of control, his telephone rings. An angry voice is heard: "Nine weeks ago, I sent you an order for three sizes of your model X-5 components. You promised seven-week delivery. As of now, I haven't received a single unit. If I don't get this shipment by the end of the week, cancel the order!"

"Well," the cautionary vignette ended, "maybe in 1966 . . ."

■ ■ ■ ■ ■

The next industry savant to raise the logistic hue and cry, after Reese, was the noted management expert Peter Drucker, who published a ground-breaking article entitled "The Economy's Dark Continent," in *Fortune* in 1962. In many respects, Drucker's logistic wake-up call echoed that of his predecessor. However, given *Fortune*'s position as the bible of American industry, his electrifying manifesto was bound to have a wider and greater impact.

It did. Interestingly, in an illustration of the increasing congruence between military and business logistics, Gus Pagonis, then a student at Pennsylvania State University, cites the Drucker article as having contributed to his logistic education.

Like Reese, it was Drucker's thesis that the hermetic, promotion-obsessed people who managed and directed the U.S. economy were, for all practical purposes, blind, by dint of their ignorance of and obliviousness to the logistic dimension of their jobs. Drucker noted that "almost 50 cents of each dollar the American consumer spends for goods goes for activities that occur *after* [my italics] the goods are made." Distribution—or logistics, as it was *then* construed to mean—was half of the ball game.

Nevertheless, the writer declared, in a much-quoted passage, "We know little more about distribution today than Napoleon's contemporaries knew about the interior of Africa. We know it is there, and we know that it is big; and that is about all." To back his charges of logistic absent-mindedness, Drucker cited a recent NYU survey of 28 putatively modern firms and what functions and business activities their CEOs considered important or significant. Fewer than half of the polled executives admitted to giving distribution or logistics any significant attention.

As a result, Drucker asserted, appearances to the contrary, the U.S. economy was not realizing its full potential.

According to Drucker, few companies think of their distributors when they speak of "their business." "Their [limited] horizons are set by the legal boundaries of their corporation." To cite one of the more glaring manifestations of corporate America logistic short-sightedness, Drucker observed that few firms either knew how large their distributors' inventories were, or, apparently, cared. The result was, well, nearly as portentous as the South Sea Bubble: "This [logistic] ignorance is a major cause of the persistent inventory booms and inventory busts that beset our economy."

Not to mention millions of dollars of lost sales from undiscovered or dissatisfied customers.

One of the problems, he noted—as had Reese—was the vague and amorphous way by which distribution was defined, with the distributive function spread out among such in-house departments as engineering, traffic, shipping, warehousing, and accounting; not to mention the distributive function assigned to the distributors themselves. With distribution dispersed, and no one in charge of the various functions and activities that came under its amorphous head, management's *visibility* of these processes—of this dark continent—was limited. Hence the CEO's field of vision and ability to maximize profits was limited, and he couldn't be a very good CEO, could he? Such was the essence of Drucker's indictment.

A related problem, according to Drucker, was the difficulty of evaluating the cost of distribution. The varying nature and definition of the logistics function group, from company to company, combined with the lack of accurate or easy-to-use computational measuring tools made it difficult to find out how much these functions cost their respective companies, further blurring them.

However, for Drucker, as for Reese, the basic reason for American business's logistic obtuseness continued to be, essentially, a matter of attitude, that is, the perception, both within the factory walls and from without, that anything associated with logistics—or shipping, as this complex function group was then commonly referred to—was unskilled or donkey work. Thus, Drucker charged, "because, to a technically minded man, most distribution work is donkey work, he tends to put a donkey in charge, more often than not a man of proven incompetence."

To be sure, Drucker noted, there were exceptions to this disheartening rule. At Sears, he noted approvingly, "every buyer is expected to know as much about the making of the product—the manufacturer, his plant, his process, his materials, his people, and his costs—as he knows about selling it in Sears stores."

But that—which was still Sears, Roebuck—was only one logistic point of light, as it were.

To Drucker, the most blatant illustration of American busi-

ness's logistics obtuseness could be seen when one opened the
door to the mercantile twilight zone known as the shipping department. "Even in the best-managed plant things change dramatically as soon as one goes through the door labeled 'Finishing
Room' or 'Shipping Department' [where] there is suddenly *a mob*
of people. Everybody seems to rush and no one seems to know
why and where." In short, all was pandemonium.—As indeed, I
was to find during my own explorations of the dark continent
three decades later.

Who knew what waste and evil lurked in the heart of the average American manufacturing firm (to paraphrase the old radio
serial, "The Shadow")?

Peter Drucker knew. And now, the readers of *Fortune* did, too.

The only way to assert control of this messy, neglected
process, Drucker insisted, echoing the logistic visionaries of the
earlier part of the century, was for businessmen to look at their
business in a new holistic way—by seeing distribution, or logistics, as an integral part of the manufacturing process, rather than
a *boring* auxiliary of it, as was so often the case.

"At a time when American business faces great competitive
pressures from abroad—especially from a unified Europe
whose industries can hold their own in technology, manufacturing knowledge, equipment and salesmanship," he continued, sounding an almost eerily prescient note, "raising the
effectiveness and cutting the costs of the American distributive
system may be a more important and more urgent job than
most managers yet realize."

And so, by building upon the basic vision of modern American marketing set forth by Archie Shaw in 1916, a vision based on
seeing distribution as the reverse side of marketing—as well as a
set of *interrelated* activities unto itself comprising transportation,
warehousing, traffic, finished goods, inventory controls, packaging *and* materials handling—Drucker helped set the stage for and

helped usher in the brave new world of what came to be called *integrated logistics management*, and the intellectual basis of what we today consider modern logistics.

"Within the last few years," said Drucker, ending on a more optimistic note than the Cassandra-like Reese, and noting the rapidly accelerating and improving state of logistic thought, "people have gained both the [logistical] perception and the tools to see the job. They have gained the perception to see systems which essentially people did not have 30 years ago, or even 20 years ago."

To be sure, Drucker's optimism about the future of distribution was well-founded, at least in part. Galvanized by his incisive analysis—as well as empowered by the new data-processing technology, which arrived in the latter part of the 1960s and which allowed them to quantify and cost their formerly "wild" (i.e., distributive) side—an increasing number of American business managers became disciples of Drucker. The onset of systems analysis helped further the idea that trade-offs between distribution activities could be achieved, which would lower operating costs without necessarily sacrificing product availability. Logistics was a funny art managers found. For example, they discovered, lower distribution costs could often be achieved via the most *palpably* expensive method—air freight, rather than by truck or rail. Perhaps there was more to this logistics thing than met the eye, after all . . .

Nonetheless, because of the persistence of the sales-fixated marketing philosophy and mentality, both within industry and in leading U.S. business schools—a problem that now two generations of business writers had identified and criticized—sadly, such logistically enlightened firms continued to be in the minority.

The root problem behind this nasty recrudescence of antilogisticianism (to coin an expression) during the 1960s—as it had proven during the 1920s, which mirrored that decade in its optimism and perception of the world as an ever-expanding universe with America at its center—was, one could say, the spirit of the Swinging Sixties itself, which, in its own memorable way, was as frothy and as superficial as was the age of Babbitt, the original, slogan-touting salesman conjured up by Sinclair Lewis in his famed 1927 novel of the same name. In the 1960s, Babbitt had morphed into the *Man in the Grey Flannel Suit*, as the equally famous novel about the archetypal, postwar—and, in this case, heroic—advertising man was called. In the booming, consumer goods-happy 1950s and 1960s Madison Avenue *ruled*.

In the world of American manufacturing this spirit translated itself into a continuing focus on sales, sales, sales. Like the 1920s, the 1960s were a fertile time for slick advertising campaigns and catchy jingles, some of which remain embedded in the American consciousness. Perhaps you remember some of them: "See the USA in a Chevrolet!" (Chevrolet); "Better Living Through Chemistry" (Dupont); "Mmm Good!" (Campbell's Soup); and so forth. Unsurprisingly, some of the most memorable jingles were associated with soft drinks: "Things Go Better With Coke" (Coca-Cola); "You Like It It Likes You" (7 Up); and so forth. Most of them have never been topped.

All well and good. Some of these products became brand names on the strength and resonance of these phrases. However, they didn't do much to promote sound business thinking or practice, and they *certainly* didn't do much to promote or enhance either the intrafirm or extra firm image or popularity of logistics or logisticians, who continued to remain in the shadow, and, more often than not, in the charge of their sales-obsessed, jingle-minded managerial overlords and colleagues.

Alas, there was nothing sexy about either the idea or even the sound of logistics; just the opposite. Do you remember any brilliant ad campaign of the 1960s mentioning anything about reliable delivery?

And so, to paraphrase Rodney Dangerfield, logistics continued to get no respect.

As we saw in the last chapter, this disrespect for logistics in the civilian sector corresponded with a similar attitude in the military one. Witness the difficulty that Joe Heiser had in Vietnam in getting respect from his immediate commander, who preferred a "fighting man" for his front-line logistics post, rather than a veteran logistician.

And so, as in the equally logistically retarded Army, and despite the manifest value and pivotal importance of logistics to the whole corporate battlefield, business logistics continued to be seen as the domain of the Shipping Room Mob, as Drucker put it. And so the big disconnect, as I call it, namely, the resistance of mainstream marketing thinking to sound, integrated logistics, and the subsequent gap between logistical thought and practice continued.

As a recent dissertation on the history of the evolution of logistics noted, this gap, bolstered by the perception that distribution work was "too applied and trade-schoolish to be part of the science and art of marketing," would continue for at least another twenty years. Indeed, as I saw during my studies at Stanford, where, even at that enlightened campus, logistics was relegated to a dusty corner of the Industrial Engineering curriculum, that gap would continue well into the 1990s.

A key factor in perpetuating this fallacious concept both of marketing and of distribution was the book which, starting in the 1960s, became the Bible of American managerial education: Philip Kotler's *Marketing Management*.

Chapter 6

Logistics and the Modern Corporate Battlefield

"People think we got big by putting stores in small towns. Really, we got big by replacing inventory with information."

—Sam Walton, founder, Wal-Mart

Logistics finally did start getting respect from corporate America in the 1970s.

This logistic enlightenment, so to speak, was propelled by the increasing realization in *some* industries—especially in the paper goods, chemical, and dairy goods industries, where only so much product differentiation was possible—that the goods they created were, essentially, homogenous, and that, consequently, the best way for firms within these industries to get the edge on their competitors was, in fact, by delivering those goods to their customers faster, better, and cheaper—and being able to document this.

This partial logistic enlightenment was also helped along

by a number of other developments, including, most notably, the increasing sophistication and availability of advanced computer technology, and with it the capacity to accurately measure inbound and outbound flow and to introduce automated inventory-flow procedures and improvements based on those measurements.

Yet another positive factor, at least at some firms, was the increasing emphasis, during the 1970s and 1980s, of the value and importance of customer service—even while a commonly accepted definition of just what that meant continued to prove elusive. At least in *some* businesses the idea that (1) customer service was important, and (2) fast, efficient, and reliable distribution of goods to the customer was a component of that idea had, indeed, begun to take hold. Correspondingly, too, the idea that logistics was a strategic function on a par with, *and* intrinsically related to, production, finance, product development, and, yes, marketing, also began to sink in. Responsibility for that function was, as Reese, Drucker, et al., had recommended, given to a new logistics superhead, or corporate quartermaster.

Nevertheless these logistically attuned and aware companies—the ones that had, under the leadership of their clear-sighted chief executives—both attained a rational, integrated vision of the various processes and flows taking place within the bounds of their walls, and had taken the requisite steps to enact and enforce that rational vision, via duly empowered logisticians, continued to be a small minority. To put it in Druckeresque terms—with a soupcon of the senior George Bush—although there were some scattered points of logistic light along the coast of America's economic Africa, the bulk of the interior, that is, the bulk of American firms, continued to stumble in the dark.

The continued, and seemingly inexplicable, imperviousness of American business to sound, integrated business practice was borne out by a 1982 *Financial Times* article whose alarmed author concluded that few companies either had or practiced a coherent plan for monitoring their own inventory. Thus, the reporter noted, only 72 out of 900 major U.S. and European firms had stock turns comparable to those attained in the frighteningly more efficient Japanese economy.

The logistical knowledge was there. So were the tools—the trained logisticians, sophisticated computer technology, and so forth.

So why, still, wasn't American industry getting with it, logistically? Why were our competitors, the Japanese, beating us at our own game, namely, the art of manufacturing?

One problem, of course, was political. It was one thing for a logistically enlightened corporate general to recognize the importance of logistics and co-equal importance of logistics with production, finance, product development, and so on. It was another to get the guys who worked in those departments to accept a co-equal logistician, or to surrender funds, authority, or personnel to him—or her (yes, there were a few female logisticians infiltrating the American corporate terrain, but just a few).

Vicious, intrafirm turf battles ensued at many such firms, preventing good logistics from being put into action. Logisticians hired to clean up the logistics mess quickly found themselves embattled, outnumbered, and, in many cases, just plain overwhelmed.

The central obstacle to logistic awareness at the unreconstructed firms, however, as numerous studies noted, remained the stubborn persistence of the same schizoid, sales-based concept of marketing which had suffused and contaminated the business environment, and had been reinforced by Madison Avenue-minded marketers for decades.

Meanwhile, Japan, the country and culture that had resisted the pull of the one-eyed king of marketing, while absorbing or aping so much else about America, had given rise to the next creative leap in business logistics: Just In Time (JIT), the notion that the most economic and efficient means of manufacture and supply was by delivering the requisite components to the factory when they were required—or just in time—for their preordained use.

It was this putatively revolutionary concept—which was cited in the aforementioned 1982 *Financial Times* article, amongst other places—that was widely seen as being behind the success of Japanese industry in surpassing its American and European counterparts, and one of the most laudable, and emulable aspects of the so-called Japanese miracle of the 1980s.

Of course, there was nothing revolutionary about JIT at all. Here again, the Japanese had proven their genius for adapting what had been originally a made-in-America idea.

The Japanese themselves were the first to admit this. "It's no secret where we learned what we do," the president of Toyota told Henry Ford II, who visited Japan in 1982 to see what he could learn about advanced Japanese business practices. "We got it from the Rouge," he said, referring to Ford's River Rouge plant.

Henry Ford must have been turning in his grave. The Japanese were using one of his own ideas to best American manufacturing, including the company bearing his own name!

Why? Why did American business continue to be in the thrall of the marketing king, when the costly and embarrassing result of this romance was so obvious? Why, so many decades after Shaw, Ford, and others had shown the way, did so many otherwise intelligent people continue to insist on doing things the wrong way?

The answer, or at least part of the answer, rested with the highly influential, and considerably wrong-headed four-P paradigm. This concept, which had been around since the 1960s and was ultimately formalized in Philip Kotler's best-selling management book, *Marketing Management*, holds that the modern day marketing manager has to understand four key principles: product, price, promotion, and place. That was it: product, price, promotion, and place. That's all you needed to know in order to manage the modern corporation.

The effect of Kotler's book, which was in its eighth edition by the time I got to it, was to perpetuate the hermetic, promotion-based marketing concept at the country's most influential business schools, and, at least by inference, to give continued credibility to the stereotype of logistics as being a secondary or impure function or process that would best be overseen by marketers, or left in the hands of the same traffic managers—or donkeys—who had continued to deal with logistics, or traffic, as this complex function was still widely understood.

Like any other sector of academe, business education was also prone to establishing an orthodoxy—even a wrong-headed orthodoxy (as most orthodoxies generally are). For the better part of four decades, that orthodoxy was based on the four-P paradigm. (An analogous development in a discipline on the other side of the campus was the way the ayatollahs of American art education fell under the spell of nonfigurative or nonrepresentational painting and drawing in the 1970s, a noxious development that had the effect of ghettoizing and marginalizing figurative drawing for the next years.)

Similarly, the obtuse four-P paradigm would continue to dominate business management culture and insure the marginalization of logistics until the mid-1990s.

In his 1992 book, *Teaching the Elephant to Dance*, James Belasco wrote about the importance of culture as both a vehicle to and obstacle to change. "Culture calls the tune," wrote Belasco. "Every organization has a way of doing things that governs virtually every aspect of working life . . . the sum total of all the standard ways people are supposed to (and actually) act. You are surrounded by culture. It's as close to you, and so second nature, that you hardly think about it."

And, until recently, American business, because of its continued reliance on Kotler—as well as the normal tendency of all cultures to resist change—continued to base itself fairly exclusively on the four Ps.

It was not until the mid-90s that this misguided mantra began to be seriously challenged—again—in print. "The marketing concept is not the be-all and end-all of management," Steven Brown wrote in *Marketing Apocalypse*. "Too many marketers are still living in a Kotlerite universe where marketing has all the answers."

And so, throughout the 1970s and 1980s, the best logisticians and logistical thinkers continued to operate in a vacuum.

Thus, as James Stock and Douglas Lambert wrote in their 1987 book, *Strategic Logistics Management*, "the acceptance of the marketing concept in the '60s and beyond by both academic and marketing practitioners led to a restricted consumer-oriented view of marketing management. This narrow focus opened a void for certain business and academic specialists to concentrate on efficiencies obtainable through improved planning and physical distribution."

■ ■ ■ ■ ■

To be sure, this void, the consequence of the continuing disconnect between logistical theory and practice, proved to be a fertile
and profitable place for some of these specialists.

One of these specialists, Keith Oliver, a London-based logistician on the staff of the management consulting firm, Booz Allen
& Hamilton, played a critical role in ushering in the next significant evolution in logistical thought.

After conducting its own surveys, the firm found that most
companies had implemented various new-fangled production-
management systems, some of them quite sophisticated and expensive, without realizing any tangible benefits.

During the late 1970s and throughout the 1980s, Oliver, who
has worked out of BAH's London office for the past 25 years,
worked with Elcoma, a subsidiary of Phillips, the Dutch electronics behemoth, which makes a wide range of electronic components. Elcoma had always found it necessary to have a large
inventory in finished stocks, mostly because of the difficulty of
forecasting demand across an extensive product range, which, at
that time included over 80,000 items.

Japanese incursions into the electronics marketplace had also
made Elcoma executives extremely nervous. They knew that reliable customer service—getting the right product to the right
place at the right time—was critical if it was to maintain its competitive position in the industry.

So Elcoma asked Oliver to have a look and see what he
could do to improve the delivery picture. "Addressing the
problem in the control systems level would have produced major emphasis on trying to improve the accuracy of demand,"
Oliver told an inquiring reporter for the *Financial Times* at the
time. "Given the characteristics of the demand—high variety

and uniqueness of the component specifications—there was a limited chance of success."

Oliver's first step was to suggest a trade-off with the customer whereby reliability of delivery would be improved in return for a marginally longer period between order and delivery. The suggested formula called for a decrease in finished stocks at the expense of a rise in semifinished stocks, because, as the consultant explained at the time, "finished inventory is three times more expensive than semifinished stocks and far less flexible."

The solution worked. Significant cost reductions were achieved. "Now we can react faster to market changes," the company's satisfied president said after the work was completed.

One of Oliver's other clients, the British cookie and confectioner Cadbury Schweppes, also decided that there had to be a better way. Cadbury had already done its best to rationalize its operations, with special attention to its confectionery division. By the mid-90s the benefits had begun to show: market share was rising, manufacturing productivity was improving, and stock levels were dwindling. Under its modernization program, management had concentrated on reducing production costs by employing fewer and more efficient machines. However, inevitably, product variety had been sacrificed. In a consumer business, where predicting demand is an endemic problem and meeting it as precisely as possible is a prerequisite to protecting market share, the traditional solution would have been to increase the same stock which management had successfully reduced over the previous 18 months.

This management was reluctant to do. Instead, Oliver was called in.

According to Cadbury, solving the problem with stock alone would have meant doubling the inventory investment from four weeks' worth of stock to eight weeks' worth. In cash terms this would have meant finding an extra $5 million, with attendant finance charges.

Taking the camera back so he could visualize Cadbury's problem as holistically as possible, Oliver discovered that the main constraint on additional capacity and flexibility was the packaging process. It was here, he suggested, that the extra investment be made. By making a marginal additional investment in new packaging machinery, Cadbury would be able to create the extra 30 percent of capacity it needed to meet the required level of customer service. And so it did.

Oliver had understood that the best way for both Cadbury and Phillips to cut their costs and regain their respective competitive edges was to look outside the box and see that both their respective internal and external units were part of one supply chain. In this way, by effecting creative trade-offs between capacity and inventory, logistically challenged companies like Phillips and Cadbury would be able to bring low cost and high value performance to their customers. And so they have.

Oliver called this holistic logistics philosophy supply chain management (SCM).

To be sure, as we have seen, Oliver's epiphany was not entirely original. Henry Ford had been there sixty years before with his pie-in-the-sky talk about a "transcontinental materials flow" that began amidst the rubber plants of Southeast Asia and ended up with the blissfully happy Ford customer driving his nifty, rubber-soled car straight into his garage. The difference between Ford's time and Oliver's was that at least some people at some firms understood what the latter was talking about. And, thanks to the computer and the instantaneous data exchange that it now allowed, realizing Oliver's version of

Ford's original vision of sixty years before was that much more feasible.

At the same time, some far-sighted American firms had been able to devise imaginative, supply chain based solutions to their problems on their own. Witness Wal-Mart, which successfully reengineered the management of the inventory of one of its standbys, Pampers diapers, with the aid of the manufacturer, Procter & Gamble.

A disposable diaper (in case you have not heard), Pampers is a bulky item that requires a lot of storage space relative to its dollar value. Historically, the mega-retailer had maintained its arsenal of diapers at distribution centers around the country (more about what exactly constitutes a distribution center in the next section). When a center's inventory would run low, Wal-Mart would react by re-ordering more diapers from Procter & Gamble.

As Wal-Mart's managers had learned, managing inventory involves an extremely delicate balancing act. On the one hand, too little inventory of a popular product, like Pampers, meant unhappy customers. Unhappy customers meant lost sales. On the other hand, too much inventory led to high financing and storage costs. Clearly, this was not donkey work. Precision was required.

With a view toward improving that aspect of its business, Wal-Mart decided to approach Procter & Gamble to see if by working together they might optimize their shared supply chain. It was evident that Procter & Gamble knew more about diaper movement through warehouses than Wal-Mart, insofar as it had information about usage patterns and reorders from its retailers around the United States.

Perhaps, Wal-Mart suavely suggested, its friends at Procter & Gamble should take on the job of actually telling Wal-Mart when to reorder Pampers for its distribution centers, as well as in what quantity. Under the proposed cooperative logistical scheme, Wal-Mart would inform Procter & Gamble how much stock it was moving out of its distribution centers to its outlets around the country. When Procter & Gamble felt that it was appropriate, it would tell Wal-Mart when and how many Pampers to reorder. If Procter & Gamble's recommendation made sense, Wal-Mart would approve it and Procter & Gamble would deliver the requisite goods.

Put another way, to use an expression we supply chain consultants are fond of, Wal-Mart had decided to break down the walls of its business. Wal-Mart had seen the light. It saw that Wal-Mart and P&G were part of the *same* supply chain!

Elementary, Archibald Shaw would have said, as would have Ford. And yet, this was just the kind of out of the box thinking that American corporate management had for decades been incapable of.

How well did the new Wal-Mart/Procter & Gamble arrangement work? Damn well. In fact, the new alliance worked so well that Wal-Mart soon suggested that Procter & Gamble skip its purchase recommendations and just ship the diapers that it thought Wal-Mart would need. In other words, as Michael Hammer and James Champy noted approvingly in their 1993 book, *Re-Engineering the Corporation*, "Wal-Mart off-loaded its inventory replenishment function onto its supplier, relocating work across organizational boundaries."

Both companies reaped advantages. As Ralph Drayer, Procter & Gamble's chief logistics officer, said, looking back, "[Procter & Gamble] saw not only lower transportation costs through better planning, load buildings, and fewer returns, but [also] lower damage, shipment surge savings, lower inventory, and importantly, higher sales."

At the same time, Wal-Mart had eliminated the excessive costs associated with maintaining its diapers inventory. The stock was managed more effectively because Procter & Gamble could do a better job of forecasting demand than the retailer. As a result, the retailer had less inventory on hand and suffered fewer out-of-stock situations. Lower inventory levels thereby freed up space in Wal-Mart's distribution centers, reducing the need for working capital to finance that inventory.

"In fact," as Hammer and Champy wrote in 1992, "[Wal-Mart's] inventory management is now so stream-lined that goods move through [its] distribution centers into stores and into the hands of customers. Whether we call this arrangement negative inventory carrying costs or an infinite return on capital, it is a wonderful state of affairs for Wal-Mart."

Another third generation SCM specialist who prospered in the academic sector of the Kotlerite void, so to speak, while significantly pushing the theoretical envelope, was my logistical mentor at Stanford, Dr. Hau Lee. Dr. Lee's logistical epiphany was something he called "the Bullwhip effect," which is how he described the effect when the balancing act between too much inventory and too little went awry, causing fluctuations in inventory levels throughout the supply chain like the "variations in reaction down the length of a whip after it is cracked." In other words, when Wal-Mart overestimated demand for Pampers, as it inevitably sometimes did, Procter & Gamble would then overestimate demand for the parts that go into making Pampers, causing grief to a company further on down the supply chain that Wal-Mart perhaps didn't even know existed—and ultimately grief to the Pampers customer, who would wind up paying for this distortion. Lee correctly concluded that cooperating and sharing proprietary information with your trading partners would alleviate the Bullwhip Effect.

The manifest wisdom and cleverness of Oliver, Lee, and other far-sighted business and academic logistical specialists, whose work was widely circulated in business journals, as well as by word of mouth—and, of course, by computer—went a long way toward breaking down the stifling Kotlerite 4P orthodoxy as the 1980s and 1990s progressed. So did the increasing imperative to cut costs.

Another important factor was commoditization, that is, the increasing role of commodity goods in our society. Commodity goods are goods that are interchangeable whether you get them from Wal-Mart or Kmart, making Wal-Mart much more successful when its supply chain is better able to get the same Pampers to you in the right quantity and assortment, with return privileges, at a cheaper price.

Meanwhile, another portentous development was taking place: the growth of what became known as 3PL, or third-party logistics, the voluntary outsourcing of a company's transportation function to an outside firm catering specifically to the logistics market. It was and is the mission of such companies, which began to proliferate at the start of the 1990s, to minimize the costs of transportation, manufacturing, inventory, packaging, and labeling. Experts at these specialist companies use computer-based models to manage and balance the multitude of factors involved in effecting these scale economies.

In 1996, as the 3PL field was mushrooming, the consulting firm of Alex Brown estimated that, nationwide, most companies could reduce their overall logistics costs by 10 percent to 40 percent. It also estimated that logistics costs accounted for no less than 10 percent of the U.S. Gross Domestic Product (GDP). According to the firm, the booming 3PL industry would be worth $50 billion by the end of the 1990s. Many scoffed at this figure, but it was correct. 3PL is significant and with corporations continuing to downsize will only continue to get bigger.

One of the pioneers in the 3PL industry (with whom I was privileged to work) was and is Ryder. Long a force in customer truck rental, Ryder had been caught in a costly and destructive spending war with archrival U-Haul. Despite spending some $200 million a year since 1993 on trucks, system upgrades, and a central-reservation system, the hoped-for payoff in profits never came. As a result, in 1996, then CEO Anthony Burns decided to sell off the truck division and exploit the growing market in 3PL. It was a smart move. As *Business Week* noted approvingly, Ryder had "seized the [logistical] moment." By the end of the decade, Ryder was the biggest player in the game.

Amidst all this hubbub, I had a logistical epiphany of my own, the last stop on the way to attaining the Tri-Level View.

You will recall from Chapter 4, I realized that the principles that exist locally inside a warehouse are the same that exist between warehouses.

Then, one evening, as I sat in a Mexican restaurant, fidgeting with sugar packets as I waited to be served, it dawned on me that there are only four things one can do with sugar packets—or any movable objects, for that matter. They can either be moved across the table—*transferred*; they could be left in the same place—*buffered*; they could be placed in a jar or container with other packets—*reconfigured*; or they could be stamped with my name on the side—*modified*. Every time I did anything to the packets, their properties changed: The costs associated with them changed, the time associated with them changed, and their configuration changed. Or, to put it in pie terms—I am a big fan of pies—the logistics challenge facing me, or anyone, or any company, was a three-layer pie, with a *physical* layer on top comprising facilities, transportation, equipment, and inventory; an *information* layer on the bottom comprising cost, time, location, configuration, and characteristics; and a *services* layer in between and uniting the activities of transferring, buffering, reconfiguring, and modifying.

I had obtained the Tri-Level View.

SECTION II

CRACKING THE CODE AND APPLYING THE CODE

Chapter 7

Getting Ready for the View

"The customer is never wrong."
—Cesar Ritz, proprietor of the Ritz Hotel, London

Presumably, by now you have been persuaded that logistics has a great history of its own, that logistics is important, that logistics is indeed essential.

You're now ready to obtain the view. You are ready to crack the code of your company's logistical problems.

Fine.

But first, ask yourself: Do you know your company?

Do you know what your company's global objectives are? To increase profits? Cut costs? Improve market share? All the above?

Most important, and you need to answer this question before you can answer any of the above: Do you know who your customers are?

Know your customers. Note the plural. For the first thing that you need to know, whether you are a CEO or logistician is who your customers—or constituencies—are, including how many of them there are.

Take it from Gus Pagonis. You will recall that the key to Pagonis's success in the Gulf War—as with Joe Heiser's success during the Korean War—was that he framed his mission *in service terms* and he knew who he was serving. Pagonis understood that he was serving several constituencies at the same time, namely, parties whose needs and interests had to be balanced and positioned. In Pagonis's case, as we have seen, he correctly considered his troops to be his most important constituency. Other constituencies included the president and the Joint Chiefs of Staff, who framed and oversaw his principal mission to service the Coalition troops; the Saudi government, royal family, and the Saudi merchants, who helped him serve his troops and realize that mission; the media, who reported on the mission; and, of course, the people of the United States, who, after all, paid his salary.

Multiple customers, multiple constituencies.

The same goes for the civilian world.

Or, as Pagonis put it: "Yes, the [chief] customer is the soldier. The person who wins the war is the guy carrying the rifle, who overwhelms and destroys the enemy.

"By contrast," he said in an inverview, "the chief customer in the civilian world is the person who buys your product. Except that in the civilian world, as in the military, you have more than one customer. At Sears: I have the target customer, you and your wife who come into our store. But the stores are my customer, also, as a logistician."

"People don't know who their customers are," Pagonis asserts.

"A logistician can service three or four customers at the same time—*and each will have different needs* [my italics]."

What about Alan Lacy, Pagonis's boss at Sears since 2000? The same holds true of him. He has multiple customers, too, as do other CEOs. However, because of his position, his position responsibilities, and mission, his constituencies are different from his subordinate, Pagonis.

Jeff Skoll, one of the two whiz kids behind eBay, the Internet auction house, and an old friend, enlarged upon this point in a conversation on the subject of multiple customers/multiple constituencies.

"I think," said Skoll, in response to my question about who his constituencies are—or were, in his former capacity as head of eBay (Skoll is now retired)—"it depends in part on what stage your company is in. At first we [at eBay] had two main constituencies: the actual user of the [eBay] site. After that, came the employees. . . . As we grew, we added investors, initially venture capitalists, and eventually the public markets. We also added the media as a constituency."

"And then I would say we also added the government as a constituency." Innovative businesses like eBay need to interact with the government to make sure complicated regulatory issues like taxes on the Internet are fair to its customers.

"So, it's probably five groups," Skoll continued.

"The trick," he asserted, "is walking the fine line between them all."

Now, let us take a closer look at your company's chief constituencies.

■ INVESTORS

So, how can you rate a great CEO? According to Skoll, "I think if you were to put out some kinds of commonalities, I think investors want good sound planning, [they want] predictability, they want information and good reporting, and of course, they want returns on their investment."

Which of these are the most important?

"At the end of the day," Skoll said, "investors are looking for [financial] performance."

And how can investors measure that?

One effective measurement, perhaps the *most* effective one, is return on equity (ROE). If you are a CEO, chances are that you are familiar with this fiscal animal. You may well have been hired or fired on the basis of it.

In any case, this is as good a place as any to refresh your memory on it, as well as to talk about how ROE impinges on your supply chain.

Let us break ROE down schematically first:

$$\text{ROE} = \underbrace{\left(\frac{\text{Profits}}{\text{Sales}}\right)}_{\substack{\text{Profit} \\ \text{Margin}}} \times \underbrace{\left(\frac{\text{Sales}}{\text{Assets}}\right)}_{\substack{\text{Asset} \\ \text{Turnover}}} \times \underbrace{\left(\frac{\text{Assets}}{\text{Equity}}\right)}_{\substack{\text{Financial} \\ \text{Leverage}}}$$

$$\underbrace{\phantom{\left(\frac{\text{Profits}}{\text{Sales}}\right) \times \left(\frac{\text{Sales}}{\text{Assets}}\right)}}_{\text{Return on Assets}}$$

Now, *as logisticians*, seen through our particular prism, that is, the Tri-Level View, we can see that ROE is influenced as follows:

➤ Assets

First, assets, as seen in the preceding diagram.

If a CEO and his logistical point team can accomplish their mission—that is, get the right product to the customer with the use of the fewest assets, then he saves money and improves his ROE. It's as simple as that, or it should be.

What comprises assets? (1) Facilities, including distribution centers—also known as warehouses; (2) transport; (3) equipment used to move inventory around; (4) the inventory itself. We will go into more detail about these categories of assets in the next chapter.

For the sake of our discussion about ROE, please note that

the CEO's object vis-à-vis ROE is to find the minimum investment in his assets or his buildings, transports, and so forth, that translates into maximum value for the rest of the supply chain. Put another way, does he want to install long-lasting bronze pipes or will cheaper, less long-lasting aluminum do?

At the same time his objective vis-à-vis improving ROE is to find the right formula for inventory turnover. Again think of our plumbing-system analogy and how quickly water put in the system should come out, because inventory should be converted promptly into accounts receivable. From a financial perspective, this conversion of inventory into hard dollars represents the most influential driver of stock value.

Simply put, improve asset productivity, reduce inventory, and increase inventory turn.

➤ Operating Costs

Secondly, let us look at operating costs, which affect profits, as seen in the preceding diagram.

Essentially, if you get the right product to the right place at the right time, and do so with the lowest possible operating costs, i.e., fewer people, fewer overnight FedEx packages, and so forth, then you will again save money and improve your ROE.

Operating costs include the costs of operating your physical distribution centers, as well as the costs of transporting goods to and from distribution centers. In a word, your object is to reduce operating costs.

➤ Satisfaction of Demand

Third, let us examine satisfaction of demand, which affects sales in the above diagram.

What does satisfaction of demand mean? This is the part that the marketers have traditionally forgotten about. Volumes have been written about this. In our customer-friendly part of the world, satisfaction of demand means getting the right product to the right place at the right time.

The secret to satisfying demand in our increasingly commoditized world, is for the customer to be *so* pleased both with the product and with the manner in which it is delivered that he or she conceives of the product *as a service*, or a product/service, that is, a product with service built into it. In other words, so much of that experience relies upon delivery that this aspect *becomes part of the consumer experience*.

Service includes frills or customer surprises. One example of a frill that I personally liked and appreciated and that solidified my attachment to Dell was the e-mails the company sent me after I ordered a computer, which kept me informed about delivery status. Another was the brand new blue Bug that Volkswagen delivered to a friend's door after his purchase of the car, along with a dozen roses and a congratulatory balloon.

Indeed, there are all kinds of ways to satisfy customer demand, once you put your mind to it.

And your investors are bound to approve because increasing satisfaction of demand will ultimately increase sales, which, as we see, will improve ROE.

Of course, how to simultaneously minimize your company's assets and operating costs and maximize your ability to satisfy demand is the billion-dollar question. It is important to keep in mind that ROE is unique to every company's individual supply chain, and is itself limited by how good a company's accounting principles are.

At any rate, while keeping in mind the other commonalities that Jeff Skoll mentioned earlier, ROE is a good working formula for measuring how you are satisfying your investor constituency.

■ EMPLOYEES

Now, let us examine how to satisfy your next constituency, your employees.

Once again, let us take a look at how Gus Pagonis treated his troops both in the military and the civilian sector. As he noted earlier, he considered both the logistical support troops—including his Ghostbusters—who were part of his command, as well as the larger body of troops assigned to the theater as his customers. He considered their needs as whole human beings. He knew from his experience in Vietnam how important it was for fighting men to have fresh fruit and vegetables. So, getting these things to the troops during the Gulf War became a priority.

The "wolfmobile," as Pagonis called it, a mobile canteen for front-line troops—and one of his most beloved innovations, came directly out of this concern for his troops' needs.

As senior vice president of supply chain management at Sears, Pagonis has continued to care for his employees and treat them as humanely and decently as possible, just as he did with his troops in Desert Storm. In his talks with me he kept referring to his subordinates as his "associates." Why? First, it's the way the man is: Gus Pagonis is a regular guy.

But it also happens to be good business, and good logistics. Satisfied employees are more likely to deliver the goods, which will increase sales, which will increase ROE.

Beginning to get the picture?

■ TRADING PARTNERS AND END CONSUMERS

Your next group of constituents, as CEO, are your trading partners and end consumers, both of whom are grouped together because they commonly stand in the same direction, and often fill the same shoes.

In respect to his trading partners, Pagonis again refers to his experience in the Gulf War: "For the first four months I had very few military people," he says. "I only had a third country host nation to support everybody. . . . Since the enemy was poised and ready to attack, it was very important [for us to have] combat troops flying in on planes and not logisticians. So [for] my first three months I commanded a paramilitary logistics organization. I took a military officer and put him in charge of 30, 50, 60, 100 Pakistani [drivers] in trucks." It is interesting to mention in this wartime context, as long as the United States is again at war, that one of Osama Bin Laden's abiding grievances with the United States has been the continuing presence of American troops on Saudi soil and the disruption this has caused to Saudi life. And yet, somehow, when Pagonis was in the region a decade ago, he was able to work closely together with the Saudis, whose cooperation he needed to fulfill his mission because he considered them, too, as his customers.

Next let us examine the concept of end consumers. It is vital to keep in mind, here, that the product is only part of the solution for the consumer. For example, if you need to know everything possible about fishing by Friday of this week, because you are about to leave on a fishing trip, then a book about fishing from Amazon is only a part of your solution. The other part of your solution—or of satisfying demand, as professor Archie Shaw would say—would be receiving said book by Thursday so that you have proper time to read it. If the book that comes with computer software enables you to evaluate your particular fishing situation, then, obviously a computer is also part of solving your problem and your need, as is the ability of the software to work with your computer—all before your Friday fishing trip. Thus, in designing a possible book about fishing and accompanying software, I would need to consider the *total solution*, including, perhaps, a tech-support phone number and compatibility check with major hardware vendors. Put another way, satisfaction of demand, including delivery of the total solution, must be considered in the design process, so supply chain management is a part of the initial design process.

According to *Webster's Dictionary*, consumer *need* is defined as, "A lack of something, required, desirable, or useful. A physiological, or psychological requirement for the well-being of an organism. Something required or wanted; a requisite. Obligation. A condition of poverty or misfortune. To be under the necessity of or the obligation to. To be in need or want. To be necessary."

What practical measures do you need to undertake in order to find your customers' needs? Perhaps you should start by conducting a consumer satisfaction survey, including intensive, well-thought out interviews. Analyze your existing markets to see if you missed any opportunities. Analyze your consumer population's demographics to discover age or ethnic patterns. Put together focus groups to see which advertising messages your target audience prefers. And while you're at it, ask your audience how it feels about the products it uses—and, where appropriate, how quickly and accurately they are delivered. Chances are, members of your audience will tell you that prompt, reliable, and accurate delivery are high on *their* list of needs.

So, let us give them what they are asking for.

Finally, take a look at your so-called innovations, if they are in fact innovations, and consider what else your technology, material, or process could be used for. Consider what you can do to raise the quantity of sales so that the cost of your goods will come down. Take a look at what technologies forecasters see in the future, and consider how this would affect your consumers. Consider the possible positive and negative social side effects of the goods that you are delivering. Is there, for example, any new legislation in the works that will create new needs for your consumers? In short, keep your constituents in mind—all of them. That is a key principle behind delivering the goods. And it was this overarching idea that led me to formulate the Tri-Level View.

Chapter 8

Acquiring the View

"Eureka!" ("I have found it!")

—Archimedes

OK. You have reviewed your global objectives. You know who your company's chief constituencies are. You're ready to obtain the view.

First, another short primer and introduction on supply chain management.

Within an enterprise—any enterprise—the supply chain is your delivery system. It is the means by which your products can be moved from one place to another, as well as the means by which they undergo the transition from raw materials to finished goods. It is the single most important differentiating factor for a company in this new century. It defines the competitive survival criteria for any company. It is the key to creating growth and profitability. It is also the key to satisfying your customers. It is the means by which you deliver the goods.

In order to "wring the fat out of the process" (as *PC Week* put it, in an article about supply chain management), a company needs to understand that it is part of an extended enterprise—just as Wal-Mart and Procter & Gamble did, as described in the last section. You and your company officers need to look beyond the physical and political boundaries that are currently constraining and restraining you—whether you realize it or not—and break down the walls separating you and the other members of your supply chain, in a rational, easily codifiable way.

The Tri-Level View is that code.

This chapter describes that code. It helps you to see your company's supply chain from a global perspective. It establishes a common language for describing all the elements of your supply chain by developing a three-tier or tri-level view that surpasses the normal vertical boundaries that hamper business—including *your* business.

The essence and beauty of the Tri-Level View is its simplicity. I like to think that Alexander the Great would have appreciated and understood it, as would have Henry Ford.

OK. Now, for an exercise:

Hold a pen, any pen, in your hand. Note, there are only four things you can do to that pen in order for you to deliver it to me. First, you can simply transfer the pen all or part of the distance separating us. Second, you can choose to buffer the pen by keeping it in place for a period of time. Third, you can take another pen, put both pens together in a box, thereby reconfiguring the initial "pen" into a "box of pens." Fourth, you can remove the cap, and put it on the back of the pen, thus modifying the pen, however temporarily.

Four things, four processes.

There you have it: the essence of delivering the goods. That's it. Transferring, buffering, reconfiguring, modifying. Those four words describe what is happening right now to all the goods that are currently in transit in the world. Those words summarize what one tenth of the U.S. economy is about: transferring, buffering, reconfiguring, modifying. Learn those words well. They are your new logistical mantra. They are the Knowledge, the key to untangling your company's logistics. They are the code.

In the global scheme of things, warehouses tend to buffer things, or hold them in place. Aircraft or other modes of transport tend to be used for transferring things.

Now, let us look at how this schema applies to the average warehouse. As a logistical entity, the average warehouse tends to be used for the purpose of buffering goods, that is, holding them in place. However, if we make a cross-sectional view of the average warehouse we will see that all four aforementioned processes are taking place at the same time.

Within an individual warehouse, that is, *locally*, you will find, at any one time, that some goods are being transferred to shelves, while other goods are being buffered, or held in place in a holding area. Meanwhile, other goods are being reconfigured by being placed in pallets with other, similar goods; while others are being modified or changed in some way. All four things are happening in any major factory in the world.

So, you ask, what happens if, say, a sweater company shifts the sweater coloring process from a manufacturing facility to the back of the store? Matter of fact, one logistically challenged sweater company of my acquaintance did just that. The company sent uncolored sweaters directly to its store outlets, and let each store choose the color mix it wished. This is global thinking. The sweater manufacturer was *thinking globally* and *acting locally*, modifying goods in the back of the store rather than in the warehouse. This is an example of what should happen after you have attained logistical enlightenment, after you have truly seen how your company is but one link in the great extended enterprise. This is an example of what happens after you have received the View.

OK, now for the nitty-gritty: how to analyze your supply chain. Essentially, you need to break down your supply chain into three levels or layers. Layer one comprises your *physical assets*, layer two comprises *processes*, as just described; layer three comprises *measurements*. By looking at your company's supply chain from this perspective, you can go on to break down the walls that prevent you from optimizing your supply chain.

■ ASSETS: PLANES AND TRAINS AND CAROUSELS

Now, let us break down the fundamentals a little more.

First, let us zoom in on the top level of the Tri-Level View and look at your company's assets. Your assets are, well, your assets, the physical portion of your supply chain—that is, all the physical things that have anything to do with distribution or delivery. That means, principally, your warehouses (i.e., where you store your goods or do the three other things that get done to goods, as described earlier) and your means of transport: your trucks, planes, boats, dirigibles, whatever. These are your assets.

Well, maybe not dirigibles. But you get the picture.

At the same time, let us see how we can relate these assets to your global objectives. In a nutshell, what you and your logistical optimization team are aiming to do is minimize your assets, and optimize their location while maximizing the efficiency of your operations by introducing economies of scale.

Now, let us go into a little more detail about those assets.

➤ Facilities

Warehouses = Distribution Centers

Warehouses—if indeed, your company has warehouses—are distribution centers where goods pass through at maximum velocity.

So, what, exactly, are distribution centers?

Distribution centers are the point in your supply chain where stocks are held, or buffered, for varying periods of time. Holding goods in a distribution center or DC, stops or interrupts the flow of goods, adding cost to these goods. One view, held by some firms and which I share, is that distribution center costs should be avoided if at all possible. This view is due to the growing realization that a distribution center can be used to add more cost than value to products. Holding goods in a distribution center stops or interrupts the flow of goods, adding cost to these goods. Inventory at rest collects holding costs.

One way to bring added value to your customer(s) and optimize your supply chain is by efficiently and effectively staging and distributing goods while reducing or eliminating storage.

Distribution management is the component of logistics that satisfies the customer—remember, that's your basic objective, satisfying demand—by moving goods through the distribution channel as quickly and accurately as possible, as determined by production processes and product demand. DCs provide what is called a *time utility* for goods. They allow a company to service the customer with shorter lead times. This is the part of logistics that used to be called donkey work.

Under this broad definition, DCs can consist of anything or anyplace that relates to the storage of raw materials or industrial goods, spares for maintenance, or finished goods while they are in transport. They also may include specialized storage facilities, such as grain silos, tobacco warehouses, refrigerated facilities, and so forth. Bear in mind that every product that is either manufactured or grown is stored at least once in its life cycle, from point of creation or manufacture, to point of use. That soda bottle you are holding in your hand has been stored at least once—probably more than once—from the time it was bottled to the time it got to your hand. And it was stored, or buffered, in a DC.

Now, how does this all relate to the Tri-Level View?

From the perspective of the Tri-Level View, DCs are the things that do the buffering. The proximity of market oriented distribution centers to the trading partner/end consumer allows a firm to serve the customer with shorter lead times. DCs increase the time utility of your goods by broadening their time availability. In other words, they affect how your customer is able to obtain a given product when or where he or she wants it, within a given time frame.

Even while some companies are moving, often wisely, to phase out or centralize warehouses, it is important to keep in mind that the distribution/warehousing function is being used to better satisfy customers, and thereby increase competitiveness.

Here is an example: You recently discover that a local store carries diskettes with additional space on them for back-up purposes for your computer. Subsequently, you decide to buy the diskettes from that conveniently located store, rather than from a larger centralized computer store in the city center that is located a considerable distance from your place of work. The placement of the distribution center directly affected the process of satisfying your need and demand for the product.

The distribution center of today takes on a strategic role in your supply chain by serving the fundamental logistical goals of shorter lead times, lower inventories, lower costs, improved customer service levels, and added value. This contrasts dramatically with the way warehouses, or distribution centers, were viewed in the past.

In the past, warehouses were generally seen as static things—which is why they were called warehouses. Things were housed in them. Things were *kept* there. And, all too often, they were forgotten there as well, creating, all the while, a major drag on the supply chain.

Until recent years, when the first rays of logistical enlightenment began to illumine the dark continent of the American economy, as Peter Drucker memorably described it, the typical manufacturer produced stock and sold stock out of his warehouse. These primeval warehouses were assigned inventory levels of sixty to ninety days. Whatever processes were taking place under their roofs were generally taking place at a glacial pace *from the general perspective of the larger, extended supply chain.* Effectively, these DCs were deadweight.

Now, with the dawn of the new logistical age, the DC is increasingly taking on a strategic role in the battle plans of manufacturers by being employed to optimize the supply chain. The DC of today is a dynamic place, one that adds value to a product, one that plays a pivotal role in satisfying the end objective of getting the right product to the right place at the right time. It is essential to a company's productivity. It is not dead weight. It is, indeed, an asset, and corporate planners must view it as such.

Lastly, it is also well to remember that a modern manufacturing facility can and often is used as a distribution center in the sense that goods can and are modified there in such a way that value is added to them.

➤ Transportation

Basically, transportation is defined in terms of mode. By this definition there are six different modes of transportation: motor transport, air transport, rail transport, water transport, pipeline transport, and intermodal transport, or transportation combining several of the above.

Motor Transport

This is the most widely used mode of transportation in the United States and is also known as motor carriage or truck transportation.

The chief advantage of motor transport is that it offers flexible, point to point service to nearly everywhere—anywhere accessible to trucks—anytime. Other advantages of this mode of transportation include the fact that it can be specially adapted for products with special properties; for example, temperature control can be changed. It is less expensive than air transport. Finally, too, motor transportation is more flexible than rail. You and your logistics staff don't have to worry about whether your rail gauge matches that of the country or market that you are trying to conquer—as Adolf Hitler and his Wehrmacht staffers learned to their dismay after they invaded Russia in 1941 and tried to replenish their armies by running German trains over incompatible Russian track.

As an example of motor transportation's flexibility, let us say that you are in charge of a motor pool operation. Your needs for specific parts are planned in advance and communicated to suppliers across the country. Motor transportation provides the flexibility to pick up parts from each supplier at scheduled times and deliver them to a manufacturing facility when they are needed.

In sum, the cool thing about motor transport, as far as optimizing your supply chain is concerned, is that it is adaptable, relatively quick—particularly compared with rail transportation, when point of pick up to point of delivery is factored in—and cheaper than rail.

Air Transport

Air transport denotes transport by airplane or jet. In the real world, it is the fastest mode of transportation; however, the high cost of air transport limits its attractiveness. Under the category of air transportation, air freight—that is, use of an air freight service like FedEx or DHL—is the cheapest mode of air transport. Generally, air transport is used when time is a crucial factor. It is also the mode that is most often used for products that are extremely valuable and are also lightweight (shipping heavy goods by air is ridiculously expensive). By the same token, air transport is *not* attractive for conveying products that are very bulky and/or of low value.

Keep in mind that air transport is often not as time-efficient as one would think, because it includes the time consumed in transporting products to the plane and waiting for take-off, plus transporting the products to their ultimate destination. Over short distances, total transportation time may be shorter when employing motor rather than air transport.

Here is an example of when and where air transportation is economically justifiable: Suppose a television company needs a camera part. The crew needs the part as quickly as possible; until it is delivered, the company is idle. Costs accrue. In this case, the high cost of shipping the needed part by air in order to get the crew back to work is probably justifiable.

Air freight can also be economical for less expensive freight that must be transported a great distance in order to meet a specific seasonal time window, e.g., transporting apparel from, say, Malaysia to Ohio—or vice versa.

Rail Transport

Rail transport often consists of miles of railcars hitched together, and is typically used for large shipments over land.

The sheer holding capacity of a train makes it one of the most inexpensive ways to transport goods. At the same time, it also makes for unique liabilities such as breakage of fragile goods, and the often incorrect assumption on the part of shippers that the miles and miles of tracks and fleets of cars and engines will be in good condition throughout their long transcontinental stretch. Believe it or not, trains break down. When that occurs, goods don't get delivered.

Water Transport

Whether it be lakes, rivers, or oceans, water transport is the most tried and true way to transfer goods from one place to another. Unfortunately, as Alexander the Great learned the hard way—recall the little problem he had with that monsoon in India?—this form of transportation depends on the body of water over which the goods are being transported not only being accessible but traversable. Unlike rail and, to an even greater degree, air, water transport is weather-dependent. Good thing to keep in mind.

As with the rail and the pipeline (described below), water transport is best for the large quantities of bulky stuff that you want to ship as cheaply as possible, such as fertilizer or oil.

Pipeline Transport

At the moment, transport or shipment by pipeline is used almost exclusively for gas and oil. The Trans-Alaska Pipeline System, one of the longest pipelines in the world, for example, consists of a 48-inch-diameter steel pipeline that traverses 800 miles and crosses three mountain ranges and 800 bodies of water to supply the United States with a million barrels of oil each day, or nearly 20 percent of the country's domestic crude oil production.

Pipe, as this mode of transportation is simply known in the trade, is so efficient and well controlled by computers that some shippers have begun using it for other products, like foodstuffs. This trend is bound to increase in the future.

➤ Equipment

Another area of asset investment that affects ROE is logistics-related equipment, such as materials-handling equipment that is used in distribution centers, and transportation equipment. Such equipment can be manual, operator controlled, or operator assisted and includes hand trucks, carts, forklifts, carousels, cranes, and conveyor belts.

As companies have moved to rationalize their facilities (e.g., using fewer distribution centers), they have correspondingly tended to use less equipment. Less equipment equals less cost. Unfortunately, it also means fewer jobs.

Here are some of the kinds of equipment we are talking about:

Storage Equipment

Once a storage location has been assigned, goods are moved to and from this locale via either: hand trucks and carts; power-assisted devices, such as forklifts and cranes; or automatic handling systems such as conveyors.

The goods are then placed in different types of manual or automated storage devices.

Manual storage devices include such things as pallet racks, bin shelves, modular storage drawers, and mobile racks and shelves.

Automatic storage and retrieval systems (AS/RSs) rotate goods, sort them, move them up and down, and increasingly mimic the complex motions of human beings. (Some have even been known to scratch themselves.)

Note that many of the aforementioned devices have analogous counterparts in the everyday world. For example, bin shelving are those handy thingamajigs in hardware stores that are used to hold cans of paint or similar items; gravity flow racks can be found in the soda container of your local convenience store—they're the thingamajigs that cause soda cans to slide forward to replace ones that are selected from the front. Horizontal carousels are the thingamajigs in soda or candy machines that revolve to the correct location, with the thing you ordered, and so on and so forth.

The point: If you walked into the average distribution center, and looked around at the equipment in use, you would find similarities to equipment and devices used in everyday life.

Conveyors

Typical conveyors can move packages on the surface of a belt or roller. Other more complex conveyors rise at a certain point where the packages being conveyed are diverted in the direction in which they are supposed to go. Yet others read the bar codes on goods as they move along the conveyor, and automatically direct them to their ultimate destination.

Picking Equipment

Picking systems fall into two general categories: picker-to-part; or part-to-picker (now say that quickly).

Briefly, in a picker-to-part system, which is typically used with a manual storage system, the order picker walks or rides a vehicle over to the precise location where each pick is made.

With a part-to-picker system, a mechanical device brings the goods to the picker, so the picker does not need to go get them.

So much for picking equipment. Now let us move on.

Unloading and Loading Equipment

In logistics land, there are basically two pieces of equipment that can help with loading and unloading: The first one is the two-wheeled hand truck, in which—you guessed it—the designated employee pushes a hand truck into the delivery vehicle, loads the product onto the hand truck, pushes the hand truck from the delivery vehicle, and—Voila!—unloads the product onto the staging area.

Then there is the manual low-lift pallet truck, a slightly more automated truck that gives our man the power of hydraulics. To lift a pallet load, the employee pushes the forks into the pallet board openings, flicks on the hydraulic system and—presto—the pallet is successfully loaded—or unloaded.

So much for the equipment category of your assets. Now let us look at the last category of assets.

➤ Inventory

Your company's inventory itself—the goods sitting in a warehouse—are, of course, your assets as well. Just ask your accounting department. Inventory factors into ROE.

Major inventory categories include *cycle stock*, goods that are used or sold; *in process stock*, goods that are kept around for a rainy day; and *seasonal stock*, goods manufactured for use or sale at a special time of year, such as winter coats or swimwear. Finally, under this heading there is also *speculative stock*, which is stock that a person or investor buys or hoards in the hope that it will be especially valuable during a future time or emergency—like umbrellas. And that's all I have to say about inventory. For the moment . . .

Moving on:

■ PROCESSES, OR WOULD YOU KINDLY PASS ME THE BUTTER, DEAR? OR SHALL I *BUFFER* IT?

Next, let us look at the middle level of the Tri-Level View, your business processes. The four fundamental processes are the same ones I referred to before when I was describing my Mexican restaurant-sugar packet epiphany, or when I was talking about pens. Once again these are *transfer, buffer, reconfigure,* and *modify*.

Once again:

Transferring and buffering describe the two possible movements, or lack of movement, of your goods.

If your goods are being moved from one place to another, they are being transferred. It does not matter whether the goods are under the same roof, or whether they are en route from one DC to another, or whether they are en route from DC to customer. As far as the larger supply chain is concerned, they are being *transferred*.

Okay. Now, if your goods are in a static state—not being moved—they are being buffered. This is the classic warehousing function. Ever since warehouses were invented, goods have generally been stored or buffered for varying periods of time from weeks to months. Perishable goods, like milk or food, tend to be buffered for shorter periods of time. Others, like wine, are deliberately stored until, well . . . their time. There are also less obvious reasons to buffer goods, such as to speculate on the future price of your goods. For example, a farmer might hoard corn in anticipation of a drought, in which case his corn becomes *speculative stock*. Or the planning manager at a manufacturer might purchase a quantity of goods and buffer them in his warehouse in order to get a bulk discount even though he knows he will not need the goods for many months. Or the retailer might buffer perfectly saleable winter coats during the summer months, so that this *seasonal stock* can be sold next winter.

Okay. Now that you understand what transferring and buffering signify, let us talk some more about the next two processes that comprise this level of the Tri-Level View, *reconfiguring and modifying*.

If your goods are being broken apart or brought together, they are being reconfigured. Take Pampers. Pampers are manufactured and packaged in small boxes. However, when they are shipped they are reconfigured into larger boxes.

If the Pampers are adjusted in any way, they are being modified. Thus, printing images of Superman on them would be modifying them. Assembling all the parts (not that there are that many) that go into a Pampers would be modifying it. In other words, any change to the look or make-up of the diaper would be modifying it. Get the picture?

■ MEASUREMENTS: TAKING A RULER TO IT

Now let us look at the bottom and last level of the Tri-Level View, the bottom level. This is where we measure the properties of our goods as they change during the delivery process. The five fundamental measurements are *cost, time, location, configuration,* and *characteristics*.

For example, imagine a package of Pampers sitting on the shelf of a warehouse. Think of this as point A. Imagine the same box of Pampers on the shelf of Wal-Mart. This is point B. What are all the possible differences between this box of Pampers at points A and B?

The first measurably different property is *cost*, which represents the accretion of labor and transportation costs, among others. Analyzing your total costs is one key to optimally managing your supply chain. A reduction in one cost at one point of the chain invariably leads to an increase in one at another point. This makes it critical to focus on the total cost of logistics—not just the cost of reducing individual activities.

The second measurably different property is *time*. Time is important because goods often have to get from one place to another in a limited amount of time. For example, if there is a sale on Christmas trees, it is obviously important that the trees arrive before December 25. Or, to cite another instructive example, if Intel, one of the world's largest computer chip makers, is unable to deliver its latest computer chips to Dell Computers, the leading computer manufacturer, then Dell's latest computer line might need to be put on hold.

The third measurably different property which can directly affect the value of goods is *locale*. For example, ski gloves are much more valuable if they are sold at a ski resort in Aspen, than they would be at a beach resort in Waikiki. And shipping poorly located ski gloves from the Waikiki Wal-Mart back to the Aspen Wal-Mart might cost more than the gloves are worth.

The fourth measurably different property is *configuration*. In a warehouse, Pampers may be configured in packages of 5,000 because it is easier and cheaper to ship this way. But on the shelf of the store, the product is configured in packages of 24 because shoppers purchase only 24 at a time.

The fifth measurably different property between the product—whether it be Pampers, or ski gloves—at point A and point B are their respective *characteristics*. At point A your box of Pampers may be nothing more than a box of disassembled plastic and adhesive, but at point B it is a fully assembled and packaged box of diapers, complete with a price tag. Obviously, the characteristics of goods can affect how those goods need to be transported. For example, a refrigerated truck might be needed to avoid spoiling perishable goods or breaking fragile ones.

These are the five different properties of a product that change during the process of successfully delivering or distributing a product. It is the optimization of these five measurements that will result in optimal delivery, which in turn leads to a well managed supply chain. They form the crux of cracking your company's logistical code.

■■■■■

With the delivery mechanism deconstructed so that the physical assets are on top, and measurements are on the bottom, it is the business processes layer—the one in the middle—which ties the two together and clarifies them at the same time.

It is important to keep in mind that *the processes directly affect the measurements*. Transferring goods from one place to another affects the cost of the goods, the time those goods are in your supply chain, and the location of those goods. Cost, time, and location are affected whenever your goods are being transferred from manufacturer to warehouse, or from put-away zone to picking zone.

Whereas transferring goods affects the time, cost, and locale qualities of your goods, buffering them affects only time and cost. Locale, obviously, is not affected until the goods are moved or transferred to another point of the supply chain.

Reconfiguring your goods affects the goods' configuration

(obviously), along with, as always, cost and time (those two little guys add up no matter what you do).

Modifying a box of Pampers obviously affects its characteristics (along with the cost and time needed to, say, print images of Superman across the diaper's fabric).

■■■■■

Of course, breaking down the walls that prevent you from optimizing your supply chain is not merely a matter of the right analysis. That's only the start. You also have to have the right corporate team in place, headed by a logistically savvy commander in chief or Chief Executive Officer, with the same logistic *values*.

Who's the corporate team member responsible for your assets? Your quartermaster, or your Chief Logistics Officer—your Gus Pagonis—is the high-profile front man who coordinates the efforts of dozens of specialty logistics providers on both sides of your company's walls. He is the man—or woman—who is responsible for the facilities and operators needed to deliver the whole portfolio of your company's products from the suppliers' shelves to their final points of consumption in the consumers' hands. He or she is the one who can see the supply chain from a vertical perspective, the person in your organization who sees the entire supply chain. In fact, he or she is the person who truly manages your assets.

Who is responsible for your processes? Your Ghostbusters are—your generals-in-training, or their more familiar corporate counterparts, Category Managers, who also happen to be your CEOs-in-training. These managers are typically responsible for a specific product category or product line. They troubleshoot the processes specific to their products. They view the supply chain as an obstacle course made of a road of trucks and buildings that goods have to "fight through" in order to reach the consumer.

This is the horizontal perspective of a supply chain: breaking through the walls of different organizations. The goods do not care that the truck they are being loaded onto today is owned by a different company than the warehouse in which they have been stored, or buffered, in for the last month. Ghostbusters look past the who-owns-what debate also. They use the Tri-Level View to focus on the method of delivery for a single product from its initial source on the supplier's shelves to its final destination in the customer's hands. Ghostbusters are the people who, quite simply, manage your processes.

Who is responsible for your measurements? Ask your intelligence officer or your Chief Information Officer, whose responsibility, from a logistician's perspective, is to provide your corporate quartermasters with fundamental information about how assets are utilized. Remember a quartermaster is dealing with a vertical view of a supply chain, looking down on each facility as a separate entity.

He or she is also responsible for providing Ghostbusters with fundamental information about specific goods as they flow through a supply chain. Remember: Ghostbusters look horizontally across a supply chain from the perspective of specific goods as they work their way through an array of facilities.

Your information officer is the person who actually manages your ability to measure the effectiveness of your supply chain.

Putting It All Together

"Only the paranoid survive."
   —Andrew Grove, describing the basis on which
      he has long run his company, Intel Corporation,
      to the *New York Times*, 1994

OK, now that we have a handle on the Tri-Level View, let us turn to opportunities for achieving our global objectives with the Tri-Level View.

Let us start at the top of our Tri-Level View, namely, the assets layer.

And within the assets layer, let us start with distribution centers.

How many of these should you have, and where should they be located? In answering this question you need to consider trade-offs between costs for inventory, transportation, the facility itself, handling, and potential lost sales and production time. And then there's the question of whether it is better to be closer to the final end consumer, to the sources of supply, somewhere in between, or in different locations, depending on which product line we are talking about.

Once you're comfortable that your distribution centers are in the right place, how large should each warehouse be? Develop a forecast of demand for your organization's products to help you determine how much space you need.

Would a flow-through warehouse, or cross dock, help move products through the distribution center more quickly? This is different from a warehouse, where, as noted earlier, the whole point is that goods are buffered for a period of time.

Should you own all your distribution centers, or could you rent space in a warehouse owned by someone else? Consider how stable demand is for your product, and how much control you feel you need over the facility. Also consider the financial investment you are gaining versus the flexibility you need to meet your changing needs. And remember, there is always the option to hire a third party to actually operate the distribution center that you, in fact, own. These are some of the questions you should be asking yourself as you schematize, rationalize, and optimize your company's supply chain with the Tri-Level View.

There will be more questions, and hopefully, more clarity as your new prismatically clear View comes into focus. . . .

Are you a believer in a greater number of small distribution centers distributed across the markets you serve, or do you prefer fewer, larger, more centralized centers? Usually only larger firms need to consider this question. Normally, the trade-offs between these two sides of the logistical equation tend to be driven by the concentration of customers in specific regions versus their equal distribution and ability to be serviced by a single, better equipped, central facility.

More questions, more clarity. . . .

How should your distribution center be laid out? Consider how much capacity you need, how many employees you need, how productive each employee can be. At the same time, you should consider the opportunities for mechanizing the distribution process, as well as ways to maintain a consistent flow of goods through the distribution center.

As they say, you can't know the answer if you don't know the question.

Which items should be stocked in which distribution centers? In determining whether all locations should carry the entire product line, should your distribution center be limited to processing one particular product line? These are some of the other questions you and your logisticians need to be asking yourselves as you measure your company's logistical I.Q.

Now let us turn to transportation.

More questions, more factors to be considered.

Are you always going to need a full truckload to transport goods, or can you make do with less than a truckload? Should you use private or public transportation? Private carriage, as it is called, is a vehicle for adding value to goods, not a source of revenue. Wal-Mart and Pepsi are examples of private carriers. Common carriage, like UPS, is used on a piecemeal basis. Contract carriage fits somewhere in between, where for a price you can customize the contract that fits your needs.

How big a fleet do you need? Take a look at your current routes and the volume of goods you move to determine if a bigger or smaller fleet makes sense.

Can you make do with one way transportation, or is closed loop (there and back) the most economical way to go?

How much are you spending to FedEx goods back and forth? Sometimes, spending millions of dollars expediting parcels back and forth between manufacturing plants saves more than enough time to compensate for the ludicrous costs. However, more often than not, better foresight and planning can help reduce the need to overnight goods day after day.

Now let us turn to equipment.

Do you have the handling equipment you need? Oftentimes when the number of facilities and transports is reduced, so is the equipment that normally goes along with them. Be sure that your equipment is not carrying much smaller loads than it is capable of carrying, or traveling greater distances that it was designed to travel.

On to inventory. More questions, more concerns on the road to true logistical enlightenment . . .

Try the touch test to see if excessive dust is sitting on boxes in your warehouse. If so, you might have inventory that has been sitting there too long.

Have you considered establishing a quick-response relationship with your trading partners? That is a relationship in which a wholesaler or manufacturer commits himself to meet specific performance criteria in exchange for the retailer providing information about demand, and promises to prominently display the manufacturer's goods.

Why not take a look at that popular creature known in the trade as Vendor Managed Inventory (VMI)? With VMI, the wholesaler goes so far as to directly monitor and manage inventory on a retailer's shelves. The retailer gives the wholesaler access to its inventory information. In return, the wholesaler's corporate Ghostbusters, or category managers, take on the job of managing the balancing act between too much inventory and too little inventory on the retailer's shelves.

Have you considered that sovereign logistical remedy known as Efficient Consumer Response (ECR)? In this mutually beneficial logistical scenario, the wholesaler and manufacturer work closely together for the purpose of reducing the paperwork that would normally be needed in order to replenish (refresh) inventory in the wholesaler's warehouse.

Have you considered managing your inventory in a push-versus-pull manner? Pushing as much of your product on to store shelves in order to meet sales forecasts, or simply to save costs on production and shipping, is not always the best idea. Waiting for retailers to pull inventory onto their shelves could be a more efficient way to go, although this option needs to be weighed against the investment costs of managing a pull system.

Have you considered establishing a standing delivery schedule between facilities?

■■■■■

Now let us move onto the processes, or middle layer of the Tri-Level View. Here the emphasis should be on using your personnel and assets in the most productive way.

How is your labor being utilized? Watch out for high levels of absenteeism over time. Ask staff members how much time on average is wasted because of inefficient equipment, information, or procedures. Ask this question frequently to find opportunities to save time (i.e., save money).

How are your safety records? Watch out for unsafe practices in your facilities, and be sure safety equipment is where it should be.

Now let us look at transfers.

Can you reduce distances traveled or materials handled? Look to see whether goods are handled twice. Look for goods traveling excessive distances. Look for goods backtracking over the same area.

Can you reduce picking time? There are many different ways to store goods. You can put the most popular items near the front. Alternatively, you can set up specific areas for specific products.

Should you reevaluate stock location? When it comes to deciding where to put goods in a warehouse, ask yourself: Should there be a fixed location for each type of goods, or should there be a random location allocated at the time the goods are ready to be stored? Take a look at the type of goods you handle and their specific demands to help you decide.

Have you considered direct plant shipments? By having goods shipped directly to their ultimate destination, you may save the trouble of transferring goods to an interim location.

Are you comfortable with your return system? Take a look

at how you are currently handling trade-ins, repairs, and defective goods.

Now let us look at buffers.

Have you balanced your ambitions for just-in-time supply with your needs for just-in-case supply? This is a delicate balancing act. Do you want to improve customer service by having a lot of extra supply hanging around, and with contingency supply in the event of disasters? Or do you want the efficiency of only having inventory when you need it?

Have you considered smoothing? An example of smoothing is using a warehouse to hold your unsold winter inventory during the summer months. Then, when next winter comes around, your sales people are not caught off guard with nothing to sell.

Have you considered whole-order delivery? That is what happens when a company decides to hold onto an order until all the parts of the order are ready. Only then, when the order is complete, is it shipped onto the customer. Mail-order book companies often use this strategy. The book company will wait for all the books in an order to be on hand before shipping the order to the end consumer. The book company subsequently saves on shipping costs. Alternatively, the book company could immediately ship books on hand, and follow up with a second shipment of the books that needed to be special ordered.

Do you see any opportunities for product postponement? An example of this expeditious procedure would be postponing the last few steps of assembly for a product until demand for it arises. Food processing companies often postpone putting labels on cans of corn until an order is placed, because the same can of corn might be sold under six different company labels.

Now let us look at reconfiguring goods. The activities described below are all typical supply chain activities. Your optimizing opportunity here is to move these activities out of the distribution center and over to other places. For example, you might reconfigure goods on the back of the truck, or in the back of the store, or on the way from the manufacturing facility.

Have you looked at substitution opportunities? The idea of substituting one good for another, or information for inventory, comes into play here. If you need to attach two items, either tape or glue can serve your purpose. You may find that one is surprisingly cheaper and more available than the other.

Have you considered product mixing? For example, when a new shirt design is available, a store will normally want a mix of small, medium, and large versions. Your store can place three separate orders: one for three smalls, another for three mediums, and another for three larges. Alternatively, it might be easier for you as the manufacturer to configure a single mix of three small, three medium, and three large shirts. Then the store only needs to place one order.

Have you looked for break bulk opportunities? For example, a wholesaler might buy bulk containers of soap, and reconfigure the soap into smaller plastic bottles. These smaller bottles are then sold individually to local stores.

Do you see any opportunities for putting items together into a kit, or kitting? For example, a toothbrush and toothpaste can be packaged together and sold as a travel kit. Common sense. *Logistical* common sense.

Can you consolidate goods for transport? Shippers give discounts for shipping larger quantities of goods. For example, shippers often give discounts to companies that use full truckloads rather than more cumbersome less-than-truckload shipments. Look for ways to reach the shippers' threshold to achieve a discount, for example, by holding up outbound shipments until the threshold is met.

Is there a way to merge goods while in transit? Oftentimes goods are left abandoned for lengthy periods of time on the dock of a warehouse, in effect, *destructively* buffered. These "orphan" goods are left waiting for related goods to drift in at their leisure. Finally when all the rest of the shipments arrive, these are shipped to another warehouse, where they are orphaned or destructively buffered again. Not good.

Have you taken a look at the kinds of packaging your firm uses to wrap goods? This is another obvious, and often overlooked place for optimizing delivery. For example, at a certain electronics manufacturer I am familiar with, the person responsible for the packaging learned the hard way that a particular shipping box design for a new product was not surviving shipment from the manufacturing site to the intended wholesaler. It was then shipped in a deplorable state to the end consumer. The problem was only discovered after several consumers shipped the product back to the manufacturing site for repairs, where it became apparent the product was damaged.

Have you considered customized packages that help your customers make more immediate use of your product? One possibility here might be a box that helps a retailer display your product.

Finally, let us talk about modifying goods.

Have you considered moving your manufacturing or assembly activities, assuming you have them, into the distribution channel? For example, one logistically challenged sweater manufacturer of my acquaintance, after taking a closer look at its operations, found that its planning managers were misforecasting whether consumers would want more green or blue sweaters. Subsequently the manufacturer decided to forgo dying sweaters at the time of manufacture. Instead, it chose to ship *all* sweaters to the stores in a single light color. The stores could then dye the sweaters themselves as they needed. A creative solution; a *logistically* creative solution.

Have you taken a look at damaged stock and the corrosive

role it plays in your supply chain? Are your staff members rightly setting damaged goods aside? Survey your customers about damaged goods coming from your warehouses, and see if that is a problem. If it is, investigate and eliminate it.

■ ■ ■ ■ ■

Now we are ready to move on to the bottom layer of the Tri-Level View, the side of our handy logistical prism that allows you to refract and measure the effectiveness of your supply chain.

Let us look at costs first. As is so often the case, the best solution is not necessarily the most obvious one, or the cheapest. In fact, reducing costs doesn't always help you reach your objectives. Sometimes increasing costs *locally* is best for the *global* good of your company.

In their book, *Strategic Logistics Management*, James Stock and Douglas Lambert described five types of logistics costs as they relate to customer service as well as to each other: transportation costs, warehousing costs, inventory carrying costs, lot quantity costs, and order processing and information costs.

Do you know the costs associated with your current customer service levels? It is often possible to measure the direct costs of providing a certain level of customer service. On the other hand, it is also difficult to assign a dollar value to providing or not providing a certain level of service.

Do you know the costs associated with your transportation set-up, i.e., the total cost of moving goods to and from your facilities?

Do you know your warehousing costs? This is where increasing or decreasing the number of warehouses becomes important.

What are your order processing and information costs? These are all of the costs associated with processing a customer order.

What are your lot quantity costs? For example, if you buy a larger "lot" of goods, you are going to get a better discount than if you buy the goods one at a time. But at some point, you are going to wind up just storing goods that you don't need, which you bought simply in order to get the discount.

What are your inventory carrying costs? How much are you paying to store your goods each day?

Information technology can often help answer the preceding questions in an ongoing fashion.

Cost's partner-in-crime, so to speak, is time.

Have you ever bothered to find out how much time, on average, is needed to process an order? The emphasis here, obviously, must be on minimizing the time it takes to fulfill your orders.

What are the promised and actual lead times on your average order? If you find a lot of delays or partially filled orders, find out why. There could be any number of culprits, including a supplier, a distribution center or an assembly line.

Now, let us talk—again—about the location of the goods. The logistical objective here should be to minimize the time spent resolving questions about the location of goods.

Where are your in-transit goods located? Find out how in-transit problems are normally identified.

How definitively can delivery times be estimated? The more definite the delivery window, the less time people spend worrying about the location of the goods.

Also: have you brought in the bar codes and optical scanners that really help you track the location of goods through your supply chain? Do you have the inventory management software you need, to go along with those bar codes and optical scanners? As you will see in the case studies to follow, knowing where the goods are is pretty darn important.

Now, let us talk about goods configuration. Are pallets of goods being broken apart or consolidated excessively? If so, find out why, and do somethiing about it.

Conversely, are pallets of goods being broken apart too early in the flow? Or are they consolidated too late in the process? There also may be missed opportunities to get bulk shipping discounts.

Finally, let us talk about the specific characteristics of your goods.

Do the characteristics of your goods ever change in concert with changes in configuration or location? If not, find out why. The emphasis here should be on processing things in parallel or in tandem. Doing two things at once, or nearly at once, can save you cost and time.

These are general examples of ways by which you can use the power and clarity of the Tri-Level View to unlock your company's logistical code and optimize your supply chain.

OK. Now that you have your logistical glasses on, so to speak, let us see how various firms have used their Tri-Level View specifications to optimize their particular supply chains.

Chapter 10

The Kobacker Company

"Discovery consists of seeing what everybody has seen
and thinking what nobody thought."
—Albert von Szent-Györgyi,
twentieth-century German scientist

Let us take a moment and assess where you, my reader—*and customer*—and I have been so far, and where we are headed on the rest of this journey.

In the first section, you were imbued with a sweeping view of the backside, or supply side, of military history down through the ages. Among other things, we watched how Alexander the Great, arguably the world's first logistician and an archetype of managerial foresight and resourcefulness, brilliantly managed his logistics, until his armies were thwarted by one of the elements in his supply chain that he couldn't manage—the weather. We gained insight into Napoleon's flawed understanding of the logistical art, and Wellington's and Grant's brilliant, and underappreciated grasp of the same. We explored the logistics used in the two World Wars of the last century, as well as the very different logistical systems and philosophy employed by Alexander's Greek descendant, Gus Pagonis, during the Allied logistical miracle in the 1991 Gulf War. Along the way, hope-fully, you came to understand that successful wars are not only about strategy and tactics.

They *also* are about logistics. Also, and perhaps most cru-cially, you came to appreciate and understand that the same dis-tinctive qualities that define the successful, logistically astute commander-in-chief are not very different from the qualities that define the successful CEO. We also saw the skills and thinking ac-quired and developed in successful military supply chain man-agement can be easily transferred to the civilian battlefield, as evidenced by the career arc of Gus Pagonis, formerly of the U.S. Army, now "general" of logistics at Sears. The ying-yang nature of military and civilian logistics will be further underlined by one of the case studies in this section.

Next, hopefully, impressed with the historic importance of lo-gistics, or supply chain management, you came to understand my key to unlocking your company's tangled, redundant, or ineffec-tive supply chain—the Tri-Level View—including the nomencla-ture employed by those who have achieved the View.

So, you know your logistics history. You know the Tri-Level View. You know your company a little better, and, hopefully, too, your company's customers and constituencies.

Now in this section, the case-studies section, we are going to look at three different case studies in which the Tri-Level View was used to crack the code of three very different companies' very different supply-chain problems, including those of a pri-vately owned, Midwestern shoe company, The Kobacker Com-pany; a branch of the armed services, the United States Air Force; and a California-based network server company, Sun Mi-crosystems. These three cases are based on logistic assessments (a term that, incidentally, stems from the military) made using the Tri-Level View, and demonstrate three of the different possible uses of the View, as well as the benefits of a successful logistic assessment.

By the time you get through these, I hope that, to paraphrase Don Koberg and Jim Bagnall, the authors of *The Universal Traveler*, you will agree that as far as modern-day logistical problems or challenges are concerned, "the outworn method of 'worrying about it' has definitely been replaced by faster, less-frustrating and feasible techniques."

■■■■■

There are several morals to the following logistical tale. One of them is that the Tri-Level View can lead you to an unexpected place and solution to satisfy your company's chief constituency, namely, your investors. In this case, it can lead you to realize that your investors may be best served by actually selling off your company, or most of it.

Another moral is that if you look under the roof of your company you may find that it was built upon the fruits of the Tri-Level View. Payless ShoeSource, the hugely successful U.S. shoe retailer headed by much-lauded CEO Steve Douglass, illustrates this moral. A large chunk of his current state-of-the-art distribution system derives from a now-defunct, nearly half-century-old shoe company, The Kobacker Company, and its former CEO, Alfred Kobacker, who, though old-fashioned in many ways, like his company, was still savvy enough, and open-minded, to listen to the frank logistic assessment of the Tri-Level View. Kobacker allowed that same corporate diagnostic device show him how to rationalize and optimize his enturbolated supply chain. Even if it did lead him, somewhat paradoxically, to go out of business!

An odd case, but a revealing one, in the sometimes surprising annals of business logistics.

The year was 1994. The U.S. economy was coming out of a recession. Consumer spending was down. At malls and main streets across the country, sales of all sorts of consumer products were down. One of the kinds of products most affected by the turndown, as is often the case during slowdowns, was shoes. Amongst the many companies affected by the sag in sales was a privately owned, Ohio-based concern by the name of The Kobacker Company. Founded in 1960 on the all-American premise of giving its customers good value and good service, Kobacker had flourished through the postwar period and beyond, expanding, at its mid-90s apogee, to a chain of more than seven hundred stores in over thirty U.S. states.

Now, however, in 1994, it was ailing. Profits were down. Kobacker was losing business to even bigger, cheaper, and more efficient companies like Payless, the store that would eventually gobble it up.

As then CEO, Alfred Kobacker's brief was to keep his company and his legacy afloat.

Like a patient who has a vague idea of what is wrong with him, Kobacker suspected that his company's affliction had something to do with the dark side of his business, that is, its distribution system, which, because of years of incremental growth, was spread out amongst three separate distribution centers, including two in Ohio and one in California. Like most traditional warehouses, none of the three facilities were especially efficient; each center was simultaneously charged with storage, handling, and distribution of the company's product. Redundancy was inevitable.

Alfred Kobacker hoped to consolidate the company's awkward, tri-facility distribution system, and then, theoretically, to automate those facilities.

Again, we are getting ahead of ourselves.

An astute CEO, Kobacker was familiar with the Holy Grail of ROE. However, because of the poor state of the economy, especially the market for shoes, his immediate concern relating to ROE was to prevent it from going down and to avoid the potential break-up of his company. Profits were a problem. His chief constituency, his family, which had owned the company for decades, was jittery. So were his next more important constituency, his family of thousands of employees who had come to regard Kobacker as a kind of uncle figure.

To his credit, Kobacker was open and interested in a logistic assessment and what it revealed about the state of his company and its distribution system.

The first order of business—the commitment phase of the assessment—was to outline the parameters of the entire logistical rescue operation. Kobacker wanted several alternative supply-chain optimization scenarios, each revolving around the part of his company's body, that is, his three distribution centers, where he correctly surmised the chief problem—and solution—lay to his company's woes.

Using an early version of the Tri-Level View, and viewing the company from the top—or assets—level first, Kobacker understood at one glance what these were, namely: the aforementioned distribution centers and the real estate value they represented, a factor that would lead him eventually to sell them off; the chain of more than 700 retail outlets, which were divided between stores specializing in selling Kobacker's popular line of women's footwear and roughly an equal number selling several lines of shoes for the whole family; his fleet of trucks; and his total inventory of shoes. That was the top level of this crystallizing analysis.

On the second level of this initial view—the one pertaining to Kobacker's processes (remember the mantra: transfer, buffer, reconfigure, modify)—Kobacker could see everything that was going on as the shoes were *transferred* from factories in the Far East and Mexico to his California distribution center, and from Europe, India, and South America to his Ohio distribution centers, *buffered* until orders from his stores were placed, then *reconfigured* for each individual order, and *transferred* to the outlets themselves. He could also see what was going wrong, as the same transfer, buffer, reconfigure, and transfer activities were duplicated piecemeal at his three independently and manually operated distribution centers. Kobacker quickly apprehended that there was a great deal of improvement to be made on that level toward his rationalizing his business.

Finally, on the bottom level of this first diagnostic view—the information or measurements level—the one that allowed us to track the cost, time, and location of his goods within the framework of the company's entire supply chain, Kobacker could see that it was taking an average of several days to as much as a week or even two to fulfill an average order from his stores, far longer than his speedier and more logistically adroit competitors. This was unacceptable.

It certainly was an eye-opener, even if the view was not entirely a pleasant one, especially to Kobacker and his somewhat flummoxed associates.

Returning to Kobacker's Tri-Level View, it was immediately clear that his main task was to improve the total investment in his centers and trucks—his assets—while simplifying them.

Correspondingly, on the middle level—the process level—he saw that he had to improve the efficiency with which his shoes were being transferred *to* and *from* his distribution centers, and buffered and reconfigured *within* his centers, thus reducing his total operating costs.

On the bottom level—the measurements level—it was also

clear that he had to reduce the time needed to fulfill orders from the field, in order to satisfy demand.

Simply put, it was clear that Kobacker needed to reduce his asset and operating costs, while reducing the cycle for fulfilling orders. That was the conclusion we reached on the basis of the Tri-Level View.

The next step was to devise several alternative prescriptive Tri-Level Views that would accomplish the company's new logistic objectives. It didn't take long to see that the best solution was one that consolidated all distribution activity into the existing main distribution center in Ohio, thus immediately simplifying the supply chain. By shutting the other Ohio facility, as well as the one in California, Kobacker could eliminate duplicate administrative staffs and could profit from the assets sold. Doing this would also open new opportunities to consolidate shipments, which could then qualify for new bulk-shipping discounts.

Although other views with other prescriptive solutions offered other possible benefits, this was the one he liked the most; it offered the immediate opportunity to cut costs, the best possible cumulative cash flow for the company, and the welcome chance to upgrade the central Ohio center with a single state-of-the-art distribution control system. Kobacker could get what he really wanted—improved customer service and lower costs—thereby allowing him to stay in business.

And so it was done; the three centers were folded into one, taking a lot of needless coil out of Kobacker's supply chain. The time for processing an order had been successfully reduced from a matter of days to a matter of hours, and the total facility and operation costs had also been successfully reduced.

The mission had been accomplished. And the validity of the Tri-Level View had been proven.

But that was not the end of this story.

To be sure, after taking the recommended prescriptive action, Kobacker had, in fact, simplified his supply chain. One of his principal assets—his facilities—had been transformed and optimized. However, his principal means of transferring his goods to his stores—his fleet of trucks—had been untouched, as had that aspect of distribution.

Not for long. Enter the brave new world of 3PL. Having successfully moved beyond their original business of parcel shipping and truck rentals into 3PL, companies such as United Parcel Service and Ryder became aggressive and persuasive exponents of the value of outsourcing—the horrid word that has come to describe the decision and process of giving a formerly intrinsic function, like logistics, to an outside source—and successfully persuaded Kobacker that it would be more profitable to him, in the long run, if he allowed one of them to handle the transfer of shoes from his distribution centers to the outlets, rather than continue operating his own fleet of trucks.

As a direct result of the optimizing chain reaction set off by the logistic assessment and the Tri-Level View, Alfred Kobacker realized the value of those movable assets, namely, his trucks, and it was easy for him to take the next logical step in reconfiguring his company. By selling his trucks, Kobacker realized his greatest asset would clearly be his more than significant chunk of 700 stores, and the real estate value they represented. He then proceeded to sell his whole chunk of stores to his competitor, Payless.

The essence of Kobacker was thereby consumed into the Payless distribution system, which has since grown to move shoes—more than half a million across North America every single day—to nearly 5,000 stores.

Ironically, and perhaps slightly sadly, the only remaining asset of his that he did not wind up off-loading was his overhauled and—briefly—state-of-the-art distribution center in Columbus, Ohio, which the Kobacker family retained. Today it still stands as a monument, at least of a kind, to the Tri-Level View and to a successful mission for this logistical fix-it device. From there it was ready for new supply-chain challenges, including one that, figuratively, dropped out of the blue sky, from the U.S. Air Force.

Chapter 11

The U.S. Air Force

"Knowledge itself is power."

—Francis Bacon, *Meditations*

Now, let us flash forward several years to a very different sort of organizational testing ground, in a different sector of society—the military—and a case that proves the applicability and efficacy of the Tri-Level View to both the civilian *and* military sectors of America. It also proves this book's thesis about the essential interchangeability of civilian and military logistics.

Except that, and most notably, by 1996, which is when this case study takes place, the state of *business* logistics had advanced to the point where the armed services and its civilian managers in the Department of Defense had decided, at long last, that *they* might have something to learn about how to better deliver *their* materiel and personnel, from *that* side of the traditional civilian/military divide, rather than vice versa, as had generally been the case heretofore.

To be sure, by the late 1990s, there was already a fairly considerable history of military logisticians advising the civilian sector, and vice versa, and ideas from one sector percolating into the other. You will recall from the first section of this book, in which we discussed the evolution of military logistics and some of the outstanding uniformed logisticians that America has produced, how then Colonel (later General) Joe Heiser and a group of other

179

top Army supply specialists were, in 1952, asked by Sears to diagnose its physical distribution operations, as supply chain management was called then (see Chapter 5)...

Recall, too, that Heiser and his logistical comrades were taken aback by the ignorance and confusion they encountered there. "One hand didn't know what the other hand was doing," was the way the then colonel and future top Army logistician (if you recall), put it at the time, before returning to the relatively more efficient Army way of doing things.

Although many former Army logisticians did go into distribution after the war, bringing their ideas about mass logistics with them (a decidedly mixed blessing), the feeling persisted on both sides of the military/civilian divide that neither had anything special to learn from each other until well into the 1970s. As Heiser points out, in *A Soldier Supporting Soldiers*, although computers and other advanced information technology were put to especially good use in Vietnam, the tragic nature of that conflict obscured that illustration of the compatibility and interchangeability between military and civilian logistics.

By the 1980s, attitudes among the military towards their civilian counterparts, including the emerging breed of campus-based logisticians, had significantly changed, as seen in the career of Heiser's successor, Gus Pagonis. Pagonis, as you know by now, was Heiser's successor as the Army's top fighting logistician and logistical wizard behind the strikingly successful logistics behind Desert Storm. One of the first Army logisticians to obtain a graduate degree in business management, Pagonis studied at Pennsylvania State University. Pagonis gives full credit to his mentor there, Professor Robert Pashek, a leader in the emerging field of integrated logistics (see Chapter 4). Pagonis's admiration for Lashek and for his previous college teacher, Robert Coyle is evident in his memoir, *Moving Mountains*, in which he calls his teacher "a pioneer in developing an integrated approach to logistics." Remember this was during an era when most theorists and practitioners were still talking about physical distribution.

"My comprehensive approach to logistics is derived in part, from [his] broad-gauge orientation," he writes. It is hard to imagine an Army logistician of a previous era speaking in such laudatory terms about a civilian expert in logistics.

The increasing interface between business and military logistics, which has continued up until the present day, was given further momentum and legitimized by the Pentagon in 1997 with the commissioning and issuance by then Chairman of the Joint Chiefs of Staff, General John Shalikashvili, of a groundbreaking position paper, "Vision 2010," about the future of the military in the post-Cold War world. Regarded then and now as a landmark statement, the paper tried to enumerate the future of the armed services in a new world where, in contrast to the past, when there were a number of hard targets, including, principally, the Soviet Union, the enemy was now ambiguous and the need for mobile logistics capability greater than ever before.

To be sure, General Shalikashvili and the other authors of that report devoted a considerable amount of attention to the vital role of logistics in the new post-Cold War world. Sounding like the logistically astute CEO that he was, Shalikashvili envisioned a future of "total visibility of all people and materiel, *so as to instill confidence in the troops with definite information about when and where goods would be delivered* [my italics]." The logistical guesswork and improvisation of the past was unacceptable.

As the world of combat became more uncertain, the need for logistical certainty became all the more greater. The Joint Chiefs were now looking to establish *information superiority*, a phrase adapted from the aerial combat term, *air superiority*.

The former was defined by General Shalikashvili as the "capability to collect, process, and disseminate an uninterrupted flow of [logistics] information while exploiting or denying an adversary's ability to do the same." Amongst other things, this underlined the importance of updating and synchronizing the information technologies used by the various armed services. Information superiority required superior information.

The U.S. Air Force, for its part, had already begun moving to establish information superiority in the skies over its sector of the cyber-battlefield a year before "Vision 2010" was issued, in 1996, when it began upgrading its component of the Global Combat Support System, the four armed services' increasingly integrated logistical command structure. Sheila Widnall, then Secretary of the Air Force—and the first woman to head an armed service—moved further to establish information superiority for the Air Force by issuing a service-wide call and directive to "modernize and integrate combat support information systems to be responsive to Air Force needs during wartime and peacetime."—Which is where the Tri-Level View entered the picture.

Turning to the civilian sector for the help she knew she needed, Widnall recruited the civilian cyber-soldiers, including myself, to evaluate ways to upgrade the Air Force's thirty-year-old combat support information systems. The Tri-Level View was used to specifically evaluate one piece of the puzzle: warehousing software. The Air Force needed help determining how best to automate and track its vast inventory, and it needed to install the software to do the job, on what has become a nearly billion dollar project.

Starting with the top level of the Tri-Level View, the level that deals with its facilities and transportation, it was clear that the Air Force was on the cusp of being organized into ten packages of "Aerospace Expeditionary Force." Each AEF—which would take about 48 hours and 10,000 airmen to deploy—would consist of about 120 aircraft and the far-flung facilities, equipment, and inventory needed to support the aircraft in order to hit up to 200 targets per day, every day, indefinitely.

The middle level of the Tri-Level View showed goods being buffered, reconfigured, and modified at various kinds of supply depots all over the world. At the same time, it also showed aircraft flying around the world transferring goods to where they were needed. Once such aircraft reached the Middle East, or wherever they were headed, the spare parts and other cargo they carried were being transferred via parachute to individual troops in the desert, or transferred to makeshift supply depots on the ground, or even continuously buffered in the air.

In the bottom level of the Tri-Level View, showing measurements, the problem was one that had plagued America's forces in every major deployment of the twentieth century: an inability to locate goods as they flow into a theater. This, in turn, causes troops to lose confidence in their logistics system and consequently submit duplicate requests for goods, or otherwise abuse the hierarchy of command, further choking the system and promoting a cycle of "blindness." A prime example of this logistical blindness actually occurred under Gen. Pagonis's command in Operations Desert Shield and Desert Storm, when the United States shipped about 40,000 cargo containers to the Middle East, and half of those containers were needlessly buffered because people in the field could not identify their contents or final destination. The Department of Defense has since estimated that more than $2 billion could have been saved if the services could have "seen" those goods as they flowed into the Gulf. Hence the need for information superiority—and superior information.

■ ■ ■ ■ ■

Regarding the top level of the Tri-Level View, Widnall clearly needed to improve her total utilization of inventory. She was hoping to prevent needless inventory from clogging the supply system during future wartime. Remember, a logistically savvy general, or in this case an equally significant secretary of the Air Force, has foresight.

In the middle processes level of the Tri-Level View, Widnall was trying to reduce needless transfers and buffers—activities for the sole purpose of identifying the contents of a container. A logistically savvy secretary of the Air Force wants economy.

In the bottom, information level of the Tri-Level View, Widnall was trying to get more information about the location of her goods and the time needed to move the goods between any two points, thus increasing her ability to satisfy demand. A logistically savvy Secretary of the Air Force wants flexibility.

Basically, Widnall needed to get her logisticians definite information about when and where goods would be delivered, so they could broadcast the information to the supply depots, aircraft, and troops on the front line.

■■■■■

The single best prescriptive Tri-Level View for the Air Force Secretary combined the purchase of a commercial warehousing software, a unique and secure bar code system, and a hand-held scanner technology that could read these unique bar codes, along with about 25 other commercial, off-the-shelf products all being integrated together.

This meant consistent warehousing software for every supply depot and aircraft hangar. For an airman on the ground in a theater of war, this meant he or she could scan the unique bar code on the side of an air dropped pallet, and the contents of the pallet would be added to the inventory of the local region's warehousing software. Then like the U.S. Navy's Zapit system, in which ship-supply officers can find out if nearby ships have the parts they need, an airman could see whether needed parts were in a nearby air drop.

Granted there were benefits to the other Views, but this View offered the most up-to-date technology to the Air Force, with the easiest roadmap to Vision 2010, and its successor Vision 2020, while still providing the needed security and control of highly confidential inventory information.

Thanks to the foresight and innovation of Widnall, the enhanced visibility of consumer and reparable goods is today a reality in the Air Force. The first software was delivered to Maxwell Air Force Base in Montgomery, Alabama, in 1998, followed by delivery to the entire Air Force in the latter part of 2000. And as of today, more than 200 Air Force National Guard and Air Force Reserve sites around the world are sharing vast amounts of inventory information with "mother" databases on the Internet where planners at headquarters, or troops in the field, can check the status of goods while they are being transferred, buffered, reconfigured, or modified.

Moral: Supply-chain visibility, or information superiority, is vital on both sides of the civilian/military divide. The Tri-Level View can help you to achieve it.

Chapter 12

Sun Microsystems

"The battleground of the next decade will be supply
chain versus supply chain."
—Warren Hausman of Stanford
University, to the *Financial Times*, 2001

If Alexander the Great were in the computer business today—
an interesting thought—his chief nemesis, I think, or at least
one of them, would be Scott McNealy, longtime CEO of Sun
Microsystems.

Since co-founding Sun—Stanford University Network—with
a number of his Stanford classmates in the now seemingly distant
year of 1982, McNealy has been on an intensive quest to offer
the best high-end network server on the planet—the place to go,
for example, if you are an Internet auctioneer with a Web site you
want the entire planet to visit. Or a rocket scientist trying to figure ways to reach another planet.

An enthusiastic, and aggressive, amateur hockey player on
the weekends, McNealy's combativeness has carried over into the
public arena, where he is known for his tongue-in-cheek jabs at
Bill Gates of Microsoft, one of his current nemeses on the corporate battlefield, whom he has done his best to outmaneuver and
outflank with mixed success.

Like many other fighting corporate generals, McNealy is fond of the combative quote. He also is a strong believer in innovation. Here is what he has to say on that subject: "Without choice, there is no competition. Without competition, there is no innovation. And without innovation, you are left with very little."

Today, in the wake of the dot.com bubble, McNealy is faced with new rules of logistical combat. Up until recently, chief information officers were basically interested in having the best goods delivered as quickly as possible. Now they want the best goods for the least money—a slightly different playing field—but one that McNealy is prepared to play on because of his advanced logistical expertise. McNealy's expertise and his quest for global visibility have led him to establish a well-oiled network of suppliers and other trading partners, who, in an advanced form of logistical cooperation, use his network to share product and inventory information among themselves. Strategic cooperation it's called. It's the new look in supply chain management—and "General" McNealy and Sun are on the cutting edge of it.

In 1997, in the early days of the dot.com boom, Sun was selling as many servers as it could turn out for the vast numbers of Internet start-up companies, telecommunications firms, and financial services companies that had come to blanket the San Francisco/Palo Alto area.

McNealy's problem at the time, as far as logistics was concerned, was dealing with the explosive growth in his business, specifically the dozens of angry customers who were calling him up at every hour of the day wondering when the servers they had ordered would be arriving. Many were hopping mad. When a Sun customer orders one hundred Sun servers, and you are a copying machine manufacturer using each server as the brain of your most popular copier, and you have the other components that go into the copier arriving from all over the world and highly paid workers standing around waiting to build these copying machines, a delay in receiving such servers by even a few days can be very upsetting. Many of these customers were transferring their upset, so to speak, to McNealy and his team.

McNealy's main problem, at that time, before the days of strategic logistic cooperation, was insufficient logistical visibility. In order to assure a customer when his server would arrive, McNealy needed to know when the parts needed to build the server would be arriving at his *own* manufacturing facility, and he couldn't do that because *his* suppliers were having the same visibility problem. The problem went down the line. As General Shalikashvili (see previous chapter) would put it, McNealy needed information superiority and he didn't have it, with the result that a lot of his "fighters" were going down. Translation: He was losing business to his competitors.

It was vital for McNealy and his logistics staff to achieve maximum visibility within and between all the participants in his supply chain, from the various points where parts were being manufactured and were entering his logistical coil, to the point where the servers were being assembled, to the point of purchase and consumption. To paraphrase the expression used to describe the long road that toilet paper takes from the tree to the point where it is manufactured, to the point where that handy product is consumed—from stump to rump. With manufacturing and distribution facilities spread out over four countries (the United States, the United Kingdom, the Netherlands, and Japan) it was pretty difficult for McNealy to see the forest for the trees. McNealy needed to get some distance.

·····

The first matter of business, once McNealy's general problem of insufficient product visibility was diagnosed, was to clarify what a successful outcome to the project would be by delineating someone in the field who enjoyed such visibility.

Michael Dell, founder and CEO of Dell, the computer manufacturer, fit the bill nicely.

It was Dell's God-is-in-the-details understanding for his business, as well as his superior supply chain information—his microvision and his macrovision, if you will—that had made Dell and his company one of the great successes of the computer industry. A key part of Dell's successful philosophy, both then and now, was to provide as much information to his suppliers as possible, in return for the understanding that these suppliers would *always* have enough inventory on hand for him.

McNealy and Sun needed to adopt something of the same philosophy and logistical approach.

Fred Smith, CEO of Federal Express, whose logistically state-of-the-art company delivers nearly five million packages plus every business day, was also seen as a possible role model. Since setting up a highly sophisticated, yet easy-to-use Web site, which enabled FedEx customers a direct window onto the company's package-tracking database, the company had saved millions, as it has done ever since.

McNealy's team needed this sort of innovativeness at home.

■ ■ ■ ■ ■

The next order of business was to use the Tri-Level View to gather as many facts as possible about Sun's supply chain, by speaking with planning managers and line workers at Sun's distribution centers and manufacturing facilities, and by surveying suppliers and questioning salespeople.

Getting the right information meant forming the right team, the core team.

The first person this core team consisted of was a representative of the company's quartermaster, the Chief Logistics Officer, the person in overall charge of the top level of the View—the asset level—and the person responsible for the day-to-day operations as well as the overall profitability of the facilities and inventory. His approval on anything affecting supply was also needed.

Next, the category managers, the corporate Ghostbusters, were the second core members in this case, the "eyes, ears, and nose" of the team, as Pagonis would put it, who traveled to every corner of the Sun empire and reported back on logistical problems regarding the middle—or processes—level of the View.

The third member of the company's core information SWAT team obviously had to be a representative for Sun's corporate intelligence officer, the Chief Information Officer, the person who was responsible for the overall information flow at the company, and the bottom level of the View—the measurements or information level.

And so the team was able to produce a good, working Tri-Level View of Sun.

Here, briefly, is what that initial View revealed.

Beginning with the top level of the View, Sun had manufacturing facilities in the United States in California and Oregon, and overseas in England and Scotland. It also had distribution centers in California, the Netherlands, and Japan. Third-party logistics providers were being used extensively to fill in the gaps that inevitably occurred in such a far-flung delivery system. Peering closer together with McNealy, it also became clear that Sun was spending exorbitant amounts of money on unused inventory in a well-meaning but costly effort to preempt any surprise shortages of parts.

The middle level of the View indicated more problems. For example, a hard disk would be transferred from one of Sun's suppliers to a Sun manufacturing facility, buffered, then modified into a Sun server, and then transferred onto a distribution center and buffered again. From the distribution center it would then be transferred to a wholesaler or direct to a domestic or overseas consumer. Unfortunately, suppliers were expecting plenty of advance notice before new parts would be needed, so any surprises on the manufacturing line or repair line would mean all half-baked goods would be buffered in place while emergency parts were transferred via the costly FedEx service, sometimes from the other side of the world—sometimes, it turned out, from another Sun facility just down the block. That was the kind of inefficiency we discovered on that level.

Finally, on the bottom level of the View—the Tri-Level information-gathering team could simultaneously see that it was often taking several days to identify problems with goods en route.

Had a Sun supplier received the parts he needed? If so, had he or she finished preparing the goods for shipment to Sun? Had he even shipped the goods yet? If so, when? When were they due to arrive? What was the air bill tracking number for such and such a good? What was the current status of the original purchase order? The informationally challenged Sun buyers and planning managers would be juggling all these questions for hundreds of parts at the same time, with few tools to help them.

Not good.

■ ■ ■ ■ ■

The third order of business as part of the ongoing logistic assessment was for McNealy and his executive team to organize a list of the key logistical issues, grouping together those parts that were somehow related, and then prioritizing each group, until a problem statement could be drawn from the groupings with the highest priority rating.

Seen from the top tier of the Tri-Level View, it was evident that McNealy needed to improve his total investment in inventory and facilities. By doing so he would reduce needless stock without affecting server sales or repairs, and, also, hopefully eliminate the distribution centers dedicated to carrying this needless stock. Like the logistically aware CEO he was, McNealy wanted economy.

In the middle level of the prescriptive Tri-Level View, Mc-Nealy needed to reduce the buffering of goods on the assembly and repair lines due to surprise shortages of parts, while at the same time reduce the need for transferring emergency parts to the line, and by so doing decrease total operating costs.

Finally, on the bottom of the prescriptive Tri-Level View, Sun needed to reduce the time needed to identify problems with goods while they were en route, thus enabling them to better satisfy demand.

To make a long story short, Mr. McNealy needed to reduce his asset and operating costs, while reducing the time needed to identify problems.

■■■■■

The fourth order of business as part of the logistic assessment was to brainstorm ways by which McNealy could get a better view of his goods *as* they moved into his factories and onto the marketplace, in order to clarify and improve those parts of his supply chain.

To accomplish this objective, Views were drawn up which, in turn, were shown to managers in order to get feedback and in order to be able to draw up more Views. Some of these comparative Views explored what worked at this end for Dell and for FedEx. Others delved into the sort of information that was needed from freight carriers. Others were posited on getting more information from suppliers, or bypassing the suppliers entirely and going to the original source of memory chips for raw inventory information.

Next, the Views of this sort that the members of the core team found most attractive were further refined.

Even more Tri-Level Views were drawn up, centering around

the creation of an air traffic control system for Sun. In one View, all of Sun's trading partners were connected to a massive central repository of logistics information. In yet another, peer-to-peer technologies were distributed to every Sun partner all over the planet, so everyone could instantly get supply chain information from everyone else. Picture a Napster service, the once bally-hooed Internet service for swapping songs, that lets you obtain not just music but inventory information. In another View, a third party personally transmitted information from the people who needed goods to the people who had the goods. All kinds of scenarios were explored.

And in the process the Sun staff got a clearer idea of not only the company's problems, but its potential. The Tri-Level View is not just an information-gathering tool. It is a means to corporate self-empowerment.

■■■■■

The next thing to do was to select the one best View that best suited Sun's needs. The best and worst case scenario was considered for each View. Each was ranked according to its ability to affect the time needed to identify problems, as well as the operating costs within and between facilities, and the costs of the inventory Sun was carrying.

The decision was made by the core team to leverage the Internet with a central repository of inventory information that linked Sun and its trading partners in the supply chain. The View also called for using a third party logistics provider to serve as the central authority for this information network.

By developing an information network that leveraged the Internet, Sun's planning managers could get early visibility of goods as they moved towards and through Sun facilities, and they could track these goods while they were en route. This allowed the planning managers to focus on any problems as they occurred. For

Sun's grateful buyers and production managers, this meant less time spent monitoring shipments, and less grief caused by problems along the line as they occurred. It also led to less needless stock being carried around. Sun's planners, as well as its suppliers could also now share more detailed transportation, inventory, and production information, which meant more accurate and timely knowledge of each other's needs and capabilities, which in turn translated into better cooperation and greater visibility.

Simply put, McNealy could get what he wanted: happy customers and lower cost of goods sold, all of which meant increased profits for Sun Microsystems.

■■■■■

The next and final stage of putting the Tri-Level View to work for Sun involved putting together a logistical remedial plan, whereby the new visibility-enhancing technology was installed. The plan included specific requirements for developing the technology to quickly integrate Sun with its trading partners while minimizing costs on both sides, and providing room for the technology to evolve. A phased approach focused initially on integrating Sun with its key suppliers, and over the long term getting Sun's dozens of trading partners to work together to accept and employ the new technology and to work for the common good of the supply chain.

And so, under McNealy's logistical leadership, it came to pass.

The effects of Sun's seamless supply chain are impressive. Besides the extra efficiency on the assembly and repair lines—by which the average time to get parts, originally 40 days, was reduced to 3 days—Sun was able to reduce its inventory of spare parts sufficiently to entirely close two of its distribution centers without adverse affects to the lines.

Warren White is Sun's current director of supply chain management for the Americas and the beneficiary of the technology—as well as the new, logistically creative thinking. Of what he calls "Sun's Logistics Virtual Network," he says that "it is now possible to ship goods directly from suppliers to where the goods are needed, bypassing intermediate stops at distribution centers."

All systems go!

And one more thing: "The overall savings to the company have run to the multimillion-dollar level."

But that is not to be the end of the story.

In many ways, to put it in military terms, "General" McNealy has completed only Operation Desert Shield—the methodical buildup of men and material into a force that can support combat indefinitely.

Keep your eye on the wake of the dot.com bubble, as it rocks the computer industry in the corporate equivalent of Operation Desert Storm. McNealy understands that business is war, and behind every significant military or business victory—or nearly every one—is a foresighted, flexible, resourceful, and innovative logistician, or a correspondingly adroit and creative logistical mind.

Epilogue

In the beginning of this book, you will recall, I said that this book was intended as a primer on logistics, a side of the business world—as well as the military world, from which the art of business logistics has its roots—that has only recently begun to receive the respect and recognition both it and logisticians deserve.

Hopefully, reading this book has helped enhance that long overdue respect and recognition, while helping to destroy the unfair and inaccurate perception that logistics, or supply chain management as it is now known, is boring. Logistics, as you have seen, is not boring, nor is it donkey work.

In the world of business, this book's primary focus, logistics—or successful supply chain management—is truly the key to victory, and only bound to become more so. Lest you doubt this, ask the CEOs of Wal-Mart or Dell, whose much-lauded victories are due, as much as anything, to the fact that they and their planners have properly recognized and managed their respective supply chains, and have obtained the strategic cooperation of all the members of their chains—not an easy thing to do. Indeed, as emerging companies look for new ways to expand their markets, as well as reduce the cost of doing business, they will inevitably find, to paraphrase Brutus, that the answer is not in their marketing "stars," but, truly, in their logistics.

During the coming century smart logistics will increasingly become the strategic differentiator between companies that succeeded and those that fell by the wayside. Companies like Wal-Mart, Procter & Gamble, as well as others have created tremendous value for their shareholders by seeing the logistical light and embracing supply chain management as a competitive weapon. The CEOs of these and other enlightened companies understand that business is war—and that in war, as was demonstrated, logistics is *key*.

Want to talk about strategy? Fine. But first, as the leaders of these and other cutting-edge companies know, you need to be able to talk about logistics.

And you can't talk about logistics unless and until you truly understand your firm or organization's logistical code. The Tri-Level View provides the key for cracking your company's logistical code. Know it. Understand it. Apply it to your company's logistics. Apply it to your competitor's logistics. Chances are that you will be surprised, if not shocked, at the wastefulness and redundancy you will find under your roof—as well as those of your competitors.

Remember, corporate commanders: Knowledge of your outfit's supply coordinates is the key to commanding *your* sector of the corporate battlefield.

Analyze the logistics of the CEO or manager whom you admire the most. Then compare his or her logistical tactics and strategy with those of the general whom you admire the most. Note the commonalties between the two. See how both employ the time-honored principles of sound logistics: foresight, flexibility, economy, simplicity, cooperation, innovativeness. Indeed, as you have seen, business logistics and military logistics are, increasingly, two sides of the same coin.

Note, too, how the victories and successes of your logistical models can be ascribed to how well these leaders know their various customers and constituencies and serve their needs and expectations, including their need for and reasonable expectation of prompt and reliable delivery of goods, services, and supplies.

How well do you know *your* company?

What are *your* company's objectives?

Who are *your* customers?

How simple are *your* company's logistics?

Can these, like Wellington's Peninsular War logistics, be cut and spliced together like pieces of rope? Do you have the foresight of an Alexander the Great? Have you looked into the future and prepared yourself and your company for every possible contingency—including a September 11? Your company's logistics are its spine. How strong is that spine?

Do you know and serve your customers as well as Gus Pagonis served his troops-cum-customers during the Gulf War, and now continues to serve his new customer base as senior vice president of supply chain management at Sears? Is your company's supply chain management strategy worthy of its customers?

Do you enjoy information supremacy over your sector of the economic battlefield? If not, why not?

Where does your company fit into the virtual corporation of tomorrow? Have you and your planners thought about the strategic advantages—or disadvantages—of sharing information with your trading partners so as to obtain and secure such supremacy? What are the pluses and minuses of this form of logistical cooperation? Where does *your* company fit—or not fit—into the great extended enterprise? Put very simply: Are you *in* or are you *out*?

These are some of the questions you ought to be asking yourself as you prepare to put this book on the shelf.

For you officers and officer cadets out there—as well as you military buffs—this book has, hopefully, further underscored the fact that logistics is truly the hidden side of war, one that needs to be emphasized in the curricula of service academies—as well as military history books in general—even more than it already is. To paraphrase Frederick the Great, without supplies, or *knowing how to deliver supplies to the front line,* no troops—or sailors or marines or coastguardsmen—can be brave.

If you're a marketing officer, the logistical bell is tolling for you, as well. As the dazzling—and distracting—aura of the so-called "managerial revolution" of the postwar era fades away, and both manufacturers and retailers understand and accept anew the wisdom and truth of the original early twentieth-century meaning of marketing (i.e., that demand creation for a product or good constitutes but one, codependent half of an equation whose other equally important half consists of *demand satisfaction*), the managerial revolution of the twenty-first century, the real revolution, will become increasingly manifest.

What does that mean to you? It means, quite simply, that you can't market (or promise, and remember, when you market something you are implicitly promising something) what you can't deliver. Demand satisfaction, including and especially satisfying the customer's legitimate and reasonable demand for and expectation of fast, reliable, and accurate delivery of the good or service in question is just as if not more important than creating the demand for it. It's common sense, really. And, as you have seen, so much of good logistics—like good business—*is* common sense.

To be sure, as I have argued herein, accurate and reliable delivery should be—must be—an intrinsic and integral ingredient of the ware you are putting on display on television, in the newspaper, or on the Internet.

One more time: *You can't promise what you can't deliver.*

Are you up to speed on your company's logistics? Can you assure your customers of accurate, on-time delivery? How well do you know your company's "other side," its logistical side? How good is your relationship with your company's head of logistics? Familiarize yourself with his or her world. Forget the four Ps. Tune into the Tri-Level View and see how and where your operations fit into the true, logistically enlightened scheme of things. Remember: Your operations are—ultimately—effective only insofar as they mesh with your company's supply chain.

These are some parting thoughts for you marketing people out there. Remember: There is another side of the universe. It's called logistics.

All you investors out there, take another look at the company you've put your money and trust in. What sort of return on equity are you getting? And, while you're at it, how good are your company's logistics, as glimpsed via the condensing glass of the Tri-Level View? Take another, closer look at the CEO who mouths the usual platitudes at the annual stockholders' meeting. Come up with some good questions to ask him or her at the next meeting—some good *logistical* questions.

For you general readers out there, take heed. Behind every good or service you use, there is a supply chain that delivered that good or service to you. In fact, you are probably part of one or more supply chains yourself. Without getting too cosmic about this, logistics is everywhere.

In closing, I would like to say that I view the art of supply chain management as a painting that is in a constant state of becoming, with Alexander the Great, the first logistician, being responsible for the first rough outline, the new Internet technologies comprising another, more detailed layer, and the Tri-Level View yet another.

There will be other layers. But hopefully you now see the Big Picture.

Glossary

Alexander the Great, or Philip II as he was originally known, in addition to being history's first great captain, was also its first logistician. Before he arrived on the world stage in the fourth century B.C. and unleashed his merciless phalanxes on his hapless Near Eastern and Asian neighbors, military leaders did not worry unduly about how to supply their small, usually close ranging forces. However, the brilliant, impetuous, and somewhat mad (though no more than any of the other great megalomaniacs of history) Greek literally wished to conquer the world, and to a remarkable degree possessed the logistical genius to fulfill his grandiose ambitions.

Assets make up the top level of the Tri-Level View, and consist of the physical portion of your supply chain, that is, all the physical things that have anything to do with distribution or delivery. That means, (1) facilities, including distribution centers, also known as warehouses; (2) transport; (3) equipment used to move inventory around; (4) the inventory itself. Put another way, if a CEO and his logistical point team can accomplish their mission, that is, get the right product to the customer with the use of the fewest assets, then he saves money and improves his return on equity. The CEO looks to his Chief Logistics Officer to manage these assets, while the general looks to his quartermaster.

Black Box is an analogy for any company's delivery system when viewed from the outside. Goods are dropped into one end of this hypothetical box; they are delivered at the other end. Few managers really know what happens inside their respective boxes. All they know, essentially, is what they put into their boxes and what comes out, that is, what is delivered to their customers.

Bonaparte, Napoleon, the author of military history's perhaps best known maxim on logistics, that "an army marches on its stomach"—as well as one of the greatest soldiers of all time, was, nevertheless not the world's greatest logistician. Seen over the course of his military career and sweeping conquests and defeats—including, most importantly, his failed invasion of Russia— the Corsican native actually managed his logistics rather poorly. However, he does deserve credit for improving upon the dated and ineffective system of semiorganized foraging used by his French Revolutionary predecessors. He also could be innovative, as seen by his use of hard tack instead of fresh bread, of which he tried to make certain his troops had several days' supply. As a military logistician, on a scale of 1 to 10, he gets a 5 from me.

Boo.com is the much-ballyhooed London-based Net shopping service founded by Swedes Ernst Malmsten and Kajsa Leander which had a brilliant birth and a catastrophic burnout. The company, which reportedly went through more than $120 million before flaming out, had not bothered to ascertain whether the average high-street shopper really *wanted* to buy clothing off the Net (some did, most did not) or even whether boo.com's much-vaunted, multifaceted, but, ultimately, hopelessly clumsy cyber-rack even worked. It did not—and neither did boo.com. In May, 2000, less than two years after its bubbly take off, boo.com and its high-living founders returned to Planet Earth with a devastating thud, as the entire staff was fired en masse, the site was shut down and sold off, and the founders beat a hasty retreat—to write a book about their experiences.

Break Bulk is what occurs when a wholesaler buys bulk containers of soap, and reconfigures the soap into smaller plastic bottles. These smaller bottles are then sold individually to local stores.

Buffering and transferring describe the two possible movements, or lack of movement, of your goods. If your goods are in a static state—not being moved—they're being buffered. This is the classic warehousing function. Buffering the goods affects the time those goods are in your supply chain and the cost of those goods until the goods are moved or transferred to another point of the supply chain.

Category Manager is the title that refers to the emerging breed of corporate Ghostbusters, or trouble shooters, in logistics-savvy corporations responsible for the middle level of the Tri-Level View—the business processes. These marketing individuals are responsible for both *creating* demand—the first half of the marketplace challenge—and *satisfying* demand—including and especially satisfying the end customer's natural demand for speedy and accurate delivery—for a specific product category or product line. These individuals troubleshoot the business processes specific to their products. They view the supply chain as an obstacle course of trucks and buildings that goods have to "fight through" in order to reach the end consumer. This is a horizontal perspective of a supply chain—breaking through the walls of different organizations. See Ghostbusters.

Characteristics, according to the Tri-Level way of doing things—in addition to being one of the measurements to be found on the bottom level of the Tri-Level View—are the features of goods that change as they undergo the transition from raw materials to finished goods. For example, imagine a bundle of Pampers on the shelf of a warehouse. Think of this as Point A. Imagine the same bundle of Pampers on the shelf of Wal-Mart. This is Point B. At Point A this bundle may be nothing more than a box of disassembled plastic and adhesive, but at Point B it may be a fully assembled and packaged box of diapers, complete with a price tag. Obviously, the characteristics of goods can affect how those goods need to be transported. For example, a refrigerated truck might be needed to avoid spoiling perishable goods or breaking fragile ones.

Chief Information Officer (CIO) is your corporate intelligence officer, the one responsible for the bottom level of the Tri-Level View, who provides the Chief Logistics Officer (CLO) with fundamental information about how assets are utilized, and provides category managers with fundamental information about specific goods as they flow through a supply chain. Your CIO is the person who actually manages your ability to measure the effectiveness of your supply chain. See Intelligence Officer.

Chief Logistics Officer (CLO) is the title that refers to the emerging breed of corporate quartermasters who are responsible for the top level of the Tri-Level View, which deals with the physical assets that make up a supply chain. Your CLO is the high-profile front man who coordinates the efforts of dozens of specialty logistics providers on both sides of your company's walls; the man—or woman—who is responsible for the facilities and operators necessary to deliver the whole portfolio of your company's products from the suppliers' shelves to their final point of consumption in the customers' hands. He—or she—is the one who can see the supply chain from a vertical perspective. He—or she—is the person in your organization who can see and harness the entire supply chain. In fact, he—or she—is the person who actually manages your assets. See Quartermaster.

Configuration, according to the Tri-Level way of doing things— in addition to being one of the measurements to be found on the bottom level of the Tri-Level View—refers to the grouping of goods, which can affect the movement of those goods from the factory to the marketplace and to the consumer. For example, in a warehouse, Pampers may be configured in a package of 5,000 because it is easier and cheaper to ship this way. But on the shelf of the store, the product is configured in a package of 24 because shoppers purchase only 24 at a time.

Consumer in the civilian world is the person who buys your product. In the military world it is the soldier. For a consumer, obtaining the product is only part of the requisite solution. The other part of the solution—that of satisfying his demand, as the logistics pioneer Archie Shaw would say—would be getting the right product to the right place at the right time.

Cooperation, within the context of supply chain management, is the ability to secure the cooperation of other members of one supply chain (e.g., tracking inventory, etc.) in accomplishing the agreed upon objectives of the entire chain.

Cost, according to the Tri-Level way of doing things—as well as one of the measurements to be found on the bottom level of the Tri-Level View—is important to manage your supply chain. Because a reduction in one cost invariably leads to an increase in another, you need to focus on the total cost of logistics, not just the cost of reducing individual activities.

Cross Dock is essentially a distribution center wherein goods are not put away into storage racks, but are instead held in a docking area for loading onto the next leg of their journey.

Customer Service Levels are a balancing act between satisfying the demand of your customers and the costs of providing a certain level of customer service. It is difficult to assign a dollar value to providing or not providing a certain level of customer service. You should always assume that it is high.

Cycle Stock is the goods that your company uses or sells.

D-day, which stands for day of decision, is the unnamed day on which a particular military operation is to begin, and most commonly refers to June 6, 1944, when the Allies successfully invaded Normandy during World War II.

Defense Logistics Agency is the logistics superagency which, since its founding in 1961, has centralized procurement and supply operations for the Army, Navy, Marines, and Air Force, and which has gone a long way toward resolving destructive and redundant rivalry between the services. The need for centralization in military procurement was recognized after World War II, when President Harry S. Truman expressed irritation over the squabbling between the services, especially between the Navy and Air Force. However, the actual groundwork for the agency was not set in motion until the administration of John F. Kennedy and his ghostbusting Secretary of Defense, Robert McNamara.

Dell Computers is the Texas-based computer manufacturer that has used its logistics savvy to go from a small start-up that started from a Texas dorm in 1984 and grew to Numero Uno in the computer industry, which it is today. Dell's logistical calling card is providing as much information to its suppliers as possible, in return for having suppliers agree to keep enough inventory around for Dell. This is a prime example of supply-chain cooperation.

Demand Creation is the hermetic, promotion-based marketing concept concerned solely with mass selling.

Demand Satisfaction, within the context of logistics, constitutes getting the right product to the right place at the right time. Satisfaction of demand—including and especially satisfaction of the need for successful delivery—will ultimately increase sales, which will improve return on equity.

Desert Shield was the first phase of the Gulf War, lasting from August, 1990 to January, 1991, which primarily consisted of the massive, methodical six-month buildup of men and materiel masterminded by the Army's then top logistician in the theater, Gus Pagonis.

Desert Storm was the combat phase of the Gulf War, including both the initial air combat and subsequent ground combat phase, which took place between January and February, 1991.

Direct Plant Shipments refers to shipments in which goods are transported directly to their ultimate destination, to save the trouble of transferring goods to an interim location.

Distribution Centers are the points in your supply chain at which stocks are held, or buffered, for varying periods of time. Holding or buffering goods in a distribution center stops or interrupts the flow of goods, adding cost to these goods.

Distribution Management. See Supply Chain Management.

Dot.Com Bubble is the name history has given to the volcano-like failure of Internet, telecommunications, and financial-services companies at the turn of the century. Like its eighteenth-century predecessor, the South Sea Bubble, that bubble was caused by neglect of the supply side of things, as well as the short-sightedness of the sales-based marketing philosophy that governed American business for most of the post–World War II period.

Drucker, Peter, is the pioneering management expert who, in 1962, published a landmark article about business logistics—or distribution as it was then called—in *Fortune* magazine. "Distribution," he said, after pointing out that almost 50 cents of every dollar the U.S. customer spends goes for activities *after* the goods are made, "is one of the sadly neglected, most promising areas of

American business." "We know little more about distribution," Drucker declared, "than Napoleon's contemporaries did about the interior of Africa. We know it is there, and we know it is big; and that's about all."

Duke of Marlborough was the eighteenth-century British general responsible for, amongst other things, a brilliant Bavarian campaign that is considered a great example of logistical planning. The Duke himself still draws high marks from historians for his logistics, as well as for the general professionalism of his men. As one of his admirers declared, "The good order of his [Marlborough's] men, as well as the excellent condition of his horses were the direct result of his logistic genius."

Duke of Wellington, Napoleon's esteemed English military counterpart and frequent nemesis, certainly cared about logistics, and managed them consistently and well. "Strategic and military operations depend upon supplies," the great English general wrote in 1809, while he was stationed in India. "There is no difficulty in fighting, and in finding the means of beating your enemy," he wrote. "But to gain your objects, you must feed."

Economy is the ability to make most economical or efficient use of available materiel and supplies, including raw material.

Efficient Consumer Response (ECR) is a mutually beneficial logistical scenario wherein the wholesaler and manufacturer work closely together for the purpose of reducing the paperwork that would be needed in order to replenish (refresh) inventory in the wholesaler's warehouse.

Eisenhower, Dwight D., the supreme—and victorious—commander of Allied forces in Europe in World War II, was a great leader, strategist, and tactician, but, alas, a mediocre logistician. It must be recalled, in Eisenhower's logistical defense, that he commanded the largest expeditionary force in history during WWII, one which comprised the forces of both the United States, Great Britain, and numerous other nations on the invasion of Europe—an operation of unprecedented scale and complexity. Also, he won.

Employees are one of a CEO's chief constituencies. It is essential to care for employees and treat them as humanely and decently as possible. It happens to be good business and good logistics. Satisfied employees are more likely to deliver the goods, which will increase sales, which will increase return on equity.

End Consumers. See Consumer.

Equipment, in the Tri-Level View of things, refers primarily to materials and machinery in distribution centers. Equipment also figures amongst the assets on the top level of the Tri-Level View. Such equipment can be manual, operator controlled, or operator assisted hand trucks, carts, forklifts, carousels, cranes, and conveyor belts.

Exchange Function is a 1920s term for consumers and producers exchanging money for goods, both ending up better off. See Demand Creation.

Extended Enterprise is synonymous with Henry Ford's concept of an intercontinental supply chain that began with the rubber plants of Southeast Asia from whence the tires for his cars came, extended through the four walls of the plant itself, and ended up in the Ford customer's garage. It is also the way you should envision *your* enterprise.

Facilities, including distribution centers, also known as warehouses, are one of the physical assets to be found on the top level of the Tri-Level View.

Firebase is a remote military camp, typically located in an area that can only get supplies by air.

Flexibility is the ability to adapt logistic plans to constantly changing conditions.

Flow Through Warehouse. See Cross Dock.

Ford, Henry, the early twentieth century inventor and car maker, was, in his embrace of the concept of physical flow, American industry's first authentic logistician, or, if you will, the Alexander the Great of business logistics. Few industrialists better understood the meaning of the concept of extended enterprise, or, for that matter, of customer satisfaction, than Ford. In creating his great automobile factory at River Rouge, a temple of mass production if there ever was one, the innovative car builder saw his plant as the end point of an intercontinental supply chain that began with the rubber plants of Southeast Asia from whence the tires for his phaetons originated, extended through the four walls of the plant itself and ended up in the Ford customer's garage.

Foresight is the ability to plan and provide for one's own supply and transport, as well as to counter an opponent's logistics.

Four-P Paradigm asserts that the modern-day marketing manager has to understand four key principles: product, price, promotion, and place. This considerably wrong-headed marketing concept was first bruited about in the 1960s and ultimately was formalized in the best-selling management book by Philip Kotler, *Marketing Management.* At least by inference, this misleading concept has given continued credibility to the stereotype of logistics as being a secondary or impure function or process that would best be overseen by marketers or left in the hands of lowly traffic managers, rather than a strategic corporate function overseen by top-notch logistics professionals.

Genghis Khan, the ruthless thirteenth-century Mongolian warrior and commander, was a masterful tactician, cleverly separating his horsemen into tight columns before simultaneously converging on the hapless enemy from various directions. He is remembered less well as an able and resourceful logistician. Ever keeping the logistical bottom line in mind, Genghis instilled in his horsemen the importance of living frugally, as well as *moving* frugally. He has also been called the ultimate logistician because he aimed to destroy his enemy's supply base by literally destroying—murdering—his enemy.

Ghostbusters are those persons responsible for the business processes on the middle level of the Tri-Level View. These logistical troubleshooters arrange for the distribution of needed supplies, relieving people on the front line of the time-consuming chore of dealing with supply issues. They also keep upper management as up-to-date as possible on what is happening within the supply chain. They are nicknamed Ghostbusters because their job, essentially, is to report on what is there or what isn't there (i.e., phantom or disappearing supplies). A more mundane term for corporate Ghostbuster is category manager.

Grant, Ulysses S., the commander of Union forces during the American Civil War of 1861 to 1865, was a master strategist, thoroughly committed to the Union cause. Although much has been written about Grant's superior generalship, little attention has been given to his superb logistics. It was his facile use of and understanding of waterways as a strategic pivot that first brought him to the attention of the then hard-pressed Union commander, President Abraham Lincoln.

Hannibal, the redoubtable third century B.C. Carthaginian general, was another great logistician. When the Second Punic War between Carthage and Rome broke out in 218 B.C., this brave, bold, and innovative commander decided to take the fight to Italy itself. To do so, he used a novel means of bringing his men and their supplies to the Mediterranean battlefront: the elephant truck.

Heiser, Joseph, an influential mid-twentieth-century American military logistician, began his career during World War II as a planner at Allied headquarters in London and after service in the Korean War eventually became the Army's top logistician during the Vietnam War. Heiser understood one of the first principles of effective military *and* business logistics: *He knew his customer*, including the troops he served as divisional ordnance officer in Korea and the top three-star general in charge of logistics during the Vietnam War. Heiser was also the first Army logistician to use Ghostbusters.

Innovation, in the logistical world, refers to the ability to meet the logistics needs of the moment by using available resources in a new way.

In-Process Stock refers to the goods still undergoing the transition from raw materials to finished goods.

Integrated Logistics Management is the 1970s term for what we today consider modern logistics, namely the *interrelated* activities comprising transportation, warehousing, traffic, finished goods, inventory controls, packaging, and materials handling.

Intel is one of the world's largest computer-chip makers. As an example of the importance of time in a supply chain, if Intel is unable to deliver its latest computer chips to Dell Computers, the leading computer manufacturer, then Dell's latest computer line might need to be put on hold.

Intelligence Officer is the military term used to describe the officer or head officer in charge of intelligence information. See Chief Information Officer.

Intermodal Transport is the combination of two or more of the following modes of transportation: motor transport, air transport, rail transport, water transport, and pipeline transport.

Inventory is part of the physical asset portion of your supply chain, and can be found on the top level of the Tri-Level View. It refers to the goods sitting in a warehouse, such as cycle stock, in-process stock, seasonal stock, and speculative stock.

Inventory Carrying Costs are how much you are paying to store your goods each day.

Inventory Turnover. See Stock Turns.

Investors expect sound planning from a CEO. They want predictability, and they want information and good reporting. At the end of the day, however, they are looking for financial performance—which is one of the fruits of sound logistics.

Just In Case is the notion that customer service can be improved by having extra supply available, and having supply in the event of disasters for contingencies.

Just In Time is the notion that the most economic and efficient means of manufacture and supply is delivering the requisite components to the factory when they are required—or just in time—for their preordained use.

Kaiser, Henry J., the great mid-twentieth-century industrialist, was arguably the greatest logistical hero of World War II. The West Coast based shipbuilder and manufacturing genius who also built the Hoover Dam, amongst other feats, revolutionized the ship-building industry and played a major role in winning the war through his extraordinary employment of mass prefabrication.

Kelley, David, the inventor and educator, is best known as the founder and CEO of IDEO Product Development. Founded in 1978 in the heart of what would soon become known as Silicon Valley, IDEO is America's largest independent product design and development firm. Both by employing his knack for visual thinking, and linking that thinking to bona fide and real-world customer needs, Kelley has come up with such groundbreaking innovations and products as the Apple mouse, the Palm hand-held computer, Polaroid's I-Zone instant camera, and an electric vehicle charging station, amongst others. A frequent guest on TV shows about innovation, he also teaches at Stanford University's School of Engineering, where he is responsible for the Product Design Program.

Kitting is the act of putting items together into a kit. For example, a toothbrush and toothpaste can be packaged together and sold as a travel kit. Common sense. *Logistical* common sense.

Kmart is a retailer that has been greatly affected by the much more successful supply chain of chief competitor Wal-Mart.

The Kobacker Company is a now defunct twentieth-century company that flourished through the post–World War II period and beyond, expanding, at its mid-90s apogee, to a chain of more than 700 stores in more than 30 U.S. states. In 1994, it was ailing. Profits were down. Kobacker was losing business to even bigger, cheaper, and more efficient companies like Payless ShoeSource, the store that would eventually gobble it up. The logistic assessment of the company based on the Tri-Level View ultimately led the company to satisfy its investors by selling off most of its assets.

Kotler, Philip, is the chief marketing guru at the prestigious Kellogg School of Management at Northwestern University. One of the unfortunate effects of his best-selling bible of managerial education, *Marketing Management,* was to perpetuate the hermetic, promotion-based marketing concept at the country's most influential business schools, and, at least by inference, to give continued credibility to the stereotype of logistics as being a secondary or impure function or process that would be best overseen by marketers, or left in the hands of the same traffic managers—or donkeys—who had continued to deal with logistics, or traffic, as this complex function was still widely understood.

Lead Time is the amount of time that is needed from when goods are ordered until they are delivered.

Lee, Hau, is a Stanford-based supply chain management specialist best known as the author of "the Bullwhip effect," which refers to the bullwhip-like dislocation that occurs in a company's supply chain when inventory is improperly managed.

Le Tellier, Michel and Louvois, were the late-seventeenth-century French father-and-son team of war administrators who came up with two pivotal logistic innovations. Michel took the lead by calculating the ration requirements of an army, arranging for civilian contractors to supply food, and setting up a wagon train system with provision reserves. Meanwhile, son Louvois developed a new form of the magazine system, which had already been used since classical times, to ensure that frontier fortresses were well stocked with supplies that could be moved out to the armies by wagon or barge.

Liberty Ships were the hardy freighters, of which U.S. shipyards built 2,700—nearly 1,000 of them by Henry Kaiser—which the United States primarily used to transport supplies overseas during World War II.

Location, according to the Tri-Level way of doing things—in addition to being one of the measurements to be found on the bottom level of the Tri-Level View—refers to goods as they work their way through a supply chain, and can directly affect their value. For example, ski gloves are much more valuable if they are sold at a ski resort in Aspen than they would be at a beach resort in Waikiki; and shipping poorly located ski gloves from the Waikiki Wal-Mart back to the Aspen Wal-Mart might cost more than the gloves are worth.

Logbase is military parlance for *logistics base.*

Logistic Assessment is a multipart logistic evaluation using the Tri-Level View.

Logistics, as a military term, refers to the art of supplying and maintaining forces in the field.

Magazine is the military term for a place where food and ammunition are stored.

Measurements are the properties of our goods that change during delivery. These properties are represented in the middle level of the Tri-Level View. The five fundamental measurements are: cost, time, location, configuration, and characteristics. A typical CEO looks to his Chief Information Officer to manage this information, while a general looks to his intelligence officer.

Modifying is the process of permanently changing goods in order to affect the goods' movements. For example, if Pampers diapers are adjusted in any way, they are being modified. Thus, printing images of Superman on them would be modifying them. Assembling all the parts (not that there are that many) that go into a Pampers would be modifying it. In other words, any change to the look or make-up of the diaper would be modifying it.

Oliver, Keith, is a top London-based logistician on the staff of the management consulting firm, Booz Allen & Hamilton. Oliver played a critical role in ushering in the third significant evolution in logistical thought. He also gave it its name: supply chain management.

Operating Costs are all the costs of operating your business. If you get the right product to the right place at the right time, and do so with the lowest possible operating costs, e.g., fewer people, fewer overnight FedExs, etc., then you will save money and improve your return on equity.

Opportunity Cost is the cost of passing up on an opportunity to improve your supply chain.

Order Processing and Information Costs are all the costs associated with processing a customer order.

Outsourcing is the horrid word that has come to describe the decision and process of giving a formerly intrinsic function, like logistics, to an outside source.

Pagonis, William G., is the logistical "wizard"—as his superior, General Norman Schwarzkopf, called him—behind the Allied success in Operation Desert Storm. Later he was able to adapt his Army expertise to his subsequent and current position as senior vice president of supply chain for Sears, Roebuck, which hired him directly from the military in 1991.

Pallet is typically a four-foot square wooden platform for stacking and storing boxes, easily picked up and transported by forklift.

Patton, George S., was the bold, thrusting, pearl-handled revolver-toting U.S. general who rose to distinction while engendering considerable controversy, and commanded the Third Army during World War II. Such was Patton's indifference to and contempt for logisticians in general that throughout the entire 1944–1945 European campaign he only saw his G-4, or chief supply officer, a total of two times—once before he assumed command of the 3rd Infantry in August, and then again, during the last week of the war.

Payless ShoeSource is the hugely successful U.S. shoe retailer currently headed by much-lauded CEO Steve Douglass. A large chunk of his state-of-the-art distribution system derives from a now-defunct, nearly half-century-old shoe concern, The Kobacker Company, and its CEO, Alfred Kobacker, who, though old-fashioned in many ways—like his company—was still savvy enough to benefit from the frank logistic assessment provided by the Tri-Level View.

Physical Assets. See Assets.

Physical Distribution. See Supply Chain Management.

Physical Supply. See Supply Chain Management.

Point of Consumption is the point at which the goods are received by the customer.

Processes make up the middle level of the Tri-Level View, and tie together the physical *assets* of the top level and the *measurements* of the bottom level. Business processes clarify why the physical assets exist and how the measurements change. The four fundamental processes are: transfer, buffer, reconfigure, and modify. Transferring and buffering describe the two possible movements, or lack of movement, of your goods. If the goods are being broken apart or brought together, they are being reconfigured. If the goods are being adjusted in any way, they are being modified. CEOs look to their category managers to manage these processes, while generals looks to their Ghostbusters.

Procter & Gamble is the American manufacturing giant that successfully reengineered the management of the inventory of one of its subsidiaries, Pampers diapers, to aid its primary customer, Wal-Mart.

Product Mixing occurs when, for example, a new shirt design is available and a store will want a mix of small, medium, and large versions. Your store can place three separate orders: one for three smalls, another for three mediums, and another for three larges.

Alternatively, it might be easier for you as the manufacturer to configure a single mix of three small, three medium, and three large shirts. Then the store only needs to place just one order.

Product Postponement is the deliberate postponing of the last few steps of assembly for a product until demand for it arises. Food-processing companies often postpone putting labels on cans of corn until an order is placed, because the same can of corn might be sold under six different company labels.

Push/Pull are two competing ways to manage your inventory. Pushing as much of your product on to store shelves in order to meet sales forecasts, or simply save costs on production and shipping, is not always the best idea. Waiting for retailers to instead pull inventory onto their shelves is often a more efficient way to go, though as always this needs to be considered against the investments required by the two different systems.

Quartermaster is the military term used to describe the officer or head officer who is in charge of supplies. See Chief Logistics Officer.

Reconfiguring is the process of grouping or ungrouping goods in order to affect their movements. For example, it is easier and cheaper to ship large quantities or pallets of Pampers; however, consumers want to buy only small quantities or boxes. Reconfiguring your goods affects—obviously—the goods' configuration, along with—as always—cost and time (those two little guys add up no matter what you do).

Reese, Bud, was the former associate editor of *Inventory Management,* who in 1961 published the first of a series of articles in the business management press entitled "Physical Distribution: the Neglected Function." In that article, Reese estimated that, for the average firm, physical distribution consumed between 25 percent and 33 percent of each sales dollar, making it the third highest cost of doing business after labor and materials. Nevertheless, despite the manifest importance of distribution, and the lost sales caused by faulty distribution processes and mediocre distribution personnel, he declared, distribution continued to hover in a kind of corporate twilight zone, neither here nor there.

Return On Equity (ROE) is a good working formula for measuring how you are satisfying your investor constituency. Seen through a logistician's particular prism (i.e., the Tri-Level View), ROE can be influenced in three ways: by moderating your company's assets, your operating costs, and your ability to satisfy demand.

Ryder System is one of the pioneers and leaders in the field of third-party logistics. Long a force in customer truck rental, Ryder was caught in a costly and destructive spending war with archrival U-Haul during the early 1990s. Despite spending some $200 million a year since 1993 on trucks, system upgrades, and a central-reservations system, the hoped-for payoff in profits never came. As a result, in 1996, then CEO Anthony Burns decided to sell off the truck division and exploit the growing market in 3PL. It was a smart move. As *BusinessWeek* noted approvingly, Ryder had "seized the [logistical] moment." By the end of the decade, Ryder was the biggest player in the game.

Satisfaction of Demand. See Demand Satisfaction.

Sears, Roebuck and Co.—or Sears as it is now known—is a retailer that was, arguably, America's first logistically aware company. Getting the distribution message early on, Sears saw fit to assign its finest minds to it. After World War I, that war's logistical genius, General Robert Wood, was hired as vice president of logistics and later rose to become its president. Little wonder that seventy years later, the company, seeing that Lieutenant General

Gus Pagonis, the Army's chief logistician during the Gulf War, was about to retire from the military, was quick to offer him a position as its vice president.

Seasonal Stock is stock held for use or sale at a special time of year.

SHAEF was the acronym of the Supreme Headquarters Allied Expeditionary Force, the combined Allied force under the command of General Dwight D. Eisenhower which successfully invaded occupied France in June, 1944.

Shaw, Archibald, was the Harvard professor who in 1916 bravely attempted to set out a body of principles and generalities that he believed to be the preconditions for the shaping of a science of business. As the prescient Harvard don saw it, marketing consisted of two synergistically linked halves: demand creation—or what is today considered marketing—and demand satisfaction—or physical supply or logistics.

Sherman, William T., was Ulysses S. Grant's disciple and eventual successor as commander in chief of the United States Army during the Civil War. He took Grant's strategy of baseless campaigning and scorched-earth tactics to its extreme with the brutal campaign he launched from Atlanta in 1864, better known as Sherman's March. "War is cruelty," he declared, in answer to his contemporary critics. "The crueler it is, the sooner it is over." Questionable ethics, perhaps, but, certainly, sound logistics.

Simplicity is the ability or talent to make logistic plans as simple as possible, and to clearly articulate them.

Smoothing is the process which occurs when a company uses a warehouse to hold its unsold winter inventory during the summer months. Thus when the next winter comes around, its sales people are not caught off guard with nothing to sell.

South Sea Bubble is the name history has given to the volcano-like failure of the world's first great international trading company and wholesaler, the South Sea Company. Founded in 1711, it was one of the first, and arguably, the most spectacular business failure in modern history. Like most bubbles, the South Sea Bubble was attributable to a combination of logistical ignorance, hubris, and outright fraud.

Speculative Stock is stock that a person or investor buys or hoards in the hope that it will be especially valuable during a future time or emergency.

Standing Delivery Schedule is a preset schedule arrangement to minimize order processing costs between two loyal trading partners.

Stock. See Inventory.

Stock Turns is a measure of how often inventory stock runs out and more needs to be ordered, relative to sales revenue. This is a good way to measure how efficiently the goods are being buffered.

Substitution is the idea of substituting one good for another, or information for inventory. If you need to attach two items together, either tape or glue can serve your purpose. You may find that one is surprisingly cheaper and more available than the other.

Sun Microsystems is the Palo Alto–based computer concern which, since 1982, has been on an intensive quest to offer the best high-end network server on the planet. In the mid-90s, during the early days of the dot.com boom, Sun's problem as far as logistics was concerned was dealing with the explosive growth in its business. The problems surrounding this growth led to Sun's quest for global visibility, and for it to establish a well-oiled network of suppliers and other trading partners, who, in an advanced form of logistical cooperation, use the network to share product and inventory information amongst themselves. Strategic cooperation it's called. It's the new look in supply chain management—and "General" Scott McNealy and Sun are on the cutting edge.

Sun Tzu was the great fourth century B.C. Chinese military theorist who understood the importance of logistics to war. His much-quoted treatise, *The Art of War*, contains numerous rules and maxims on how to best support one's armies in the field, including, for instance, very specific ones on how much and how often soldiers are to be paid. Logistics was clearly an important aspect of the art of war to Sun Tzu, and, evidently, to the ancient Chinese generals upon whose operational experience he based his theories of warfare.

Supply Chain is the delivery system upon which an enterprise, any enterprise, relies. It is the means by which your company's products can be moved from one place to another, as well as the means by which they make the transition from raw materials to finished goods.

Supply Chain Management, the most current term used to describe the most advanced corporate logistics, holistically deals with the problems and challenges of moving goods and services from the factory to the marketplace to the consumer.

Supply Depot is a military term for warehouses that store goods, such as food, ammunition, and motor vehicles.

Theater refers to all land, sea, and air involved in a specific war operation.

Third Party Logistics (3PL) is the outsourcing of a logistically challenged company's transportation function to an outside firm catering specifically to the logistics market. It is the mission of such companies to minimize the costs of transportation, manufacturing, inventory, packaging, and labeling, and so forth. Experts at these companies use computer-based models to manage and balance the multitude of factors involved in effecting these reductions.

Time, according to the Tri-Level way of doing things—in addition to being one of the measurements to be found on the bottom level of the Tri-Level View—is important because goods often have to get from one place to another in a limited amount of time. For example, if there is a sale on Christmas trees, it is obviously important that the trees arrive before December 25. Or, to cite another instructive example, if Intel, one of the world's largest computer chip makers, is unable to deliver to Dell Computers, the leading computer manufacturer, its latest computer chips, then Dell's latest computer line might need to be put on hold.

Time Utility is the value created by making goods available at the right time.

Trading Partners principally take on the characteristics of consumers, where the product is only part of the solution. The other part of your solution—or of satisfying your demand, as the late professor Archie Shaw would say—would be getting the right product to the right place at the right time, with the right return privileges, and so forth.

Transcontinental Materials Flow. See Extended Enterprise.

Transferring and buffering describe the two possible movements, or lack of movement, of your goods. If the goods are being moved from one place to another they are being transferred. It does not matter whether the goods are under the same roof, or whether they are en route from one distribution center to another, or whether they are en route from distribution center to customer. As far as the larger supply chain is concerned, they are being *transferred*. Transferring goods from one place to another affects the cost of the goods, the time those goods are in your supply chain, and the location of those goods.

Transportation is one of the physical assets to be found on the top level of the Tri-Level View. There are six different modes of transportation: motor transport, air transport, rail transport, water transport, pipeline transport, and intermodal transport, or transportation combining several of the above.

Transportation Costs are the costs associated with your transportation set-up, that is, the total cost of moving goods to and from your facilities.

Tri-Level View is a model, or formula, for viewing a company's supply chain from a global perspective. It establishes a common language for describing all the elements of your supply chain by developing a three-tier or Tri-Level View that defies the normal vertical boundaries that hamper business—including your business. The *top level* of the Tri-Level View comprises your company's physical assets; the *middle level* comprises your business processes; the *bottom level* comprises the measurements with which you track the physical flow of your goods. By looking at your company's supply chain from this perspective, you can go on to break down the walls that prevent you from optimizing your supply chain.

Vendor-Managed Inventory refers to that logistical situation in which the wholesaler goes so far as to directly monitor and manage inventory on a retailer's shelves. The retailer gives the wholesaler access to its inventory information, in exchange for which the wholesaler's corporate Ghostbusters, or category managers, take on the job of managing the balancing act between too much inventory and too little inventory on the retailer's shelves.

Wal-Mart is the world's largest retailer, with one million employees spread across nearly 3,500 facilities internationally, servicing more than 100 million customers per week. This far-sighted American firm has been able to devise imaginative, supply chain based solutions to its problems, such as successfully reengineering the management of the inventory of one of its standbys, Pampers diapers, with the aid of the manufacturer, Procter & Gamble.

Warehouse. See Distribution Center.

Warehousing Costs are the asset and operating costs associated with your warehouse setup; that is, the total cost of buffering goods in your facilities. This is where increasing or decreasing the number of warehouses becomes important.

Webster, Richard, was the author of a particularly prescient 1929 article in *Sales Management* entitled "Careless Physical Distribution: A Monkey Wrench in Sales Machinery." In that article, the author tried to call readers' attention to the essentiality of physical distribution to sales and profits. Webster ascribed part of the problem to the lack of reliable measurements with which to track the physical flow of goods. Existing cost-accounting procedures, he pointed out, were inadequate, failing to pinpoint the real cost of excessive inventories and customer satisfaction.

Whole Order Delivery is that which takes place when a company decides to hold onto an order until all the parts of the order are ready. Only then, when the order is complete, is it shipped onto the customer. Mail-order book companies often use this strategy. The book company will wait for all the books in an order to be on hand before shipping the order to the end consumer. The book company subsequently saves on shipping costs. Alternatively, the book company could immediately ship books on hand, and follow up with a second shipment of the books that needed to be special ordered.

Wood, Robert E., was the U.S. Army's chief supply officer during World War I, who then went on to become the vice president of logistics for Sears and later president of the company.

References

Air Force. *U.S. Air Force Posture Statement* (2001).

"Aleyska Pipeline." *A Matter of Fact* (2002).

Ambrose, Stephen. *Citizen Soldiers: The U.S. Army from the Normandy Beaches to the Bulge to the Surrender of Germany*. New York: Simon & Schuster, 1997.

Bagnall, Jim, and Don Koberg. *The Universal Traveler: A Soft-Systems Guide to Creativity, Problem-Solving and the Process of Reaching Goals*. Menlo Park: Crisp Publications, 1991.

Baxter, A. "Understanding Supply Chain Management." *Financial Times* (November 13, 2001).

Belasco, James. *Teaching the Elephant to Dance*. New York: Plume, 1991.

Bellman, Eric. "The Crucial, Humdrum Business of Keeping Forces Supplied." *Wall Street Journal* (October 31, 2001).

Berman, Dennis. "Lousy Forecasts Helped Fuel the Telecom Mess." *Wall Street Journal* (July 9, 2001).

Berner, Robert. "Federated's Fingerhut Fiasco." *BusinessWeek* (December 18, 2000).

Boehm, Robert E., of Deloitte and Touche, interview with Damon Schechter (December 12, 2001).

Borden, N. "The Concept of the Marketing Mix." *Journal of Advertising Research* (June 1964).

Bowersox, Donald J., and J. D. Patricia. *Leading Edge Logistics: Competitive Positioning for the 1990s*. Oak Brook, IL: Council of Logistics Management, 1989.

Brown, Stephen, Jim Bell, and David Carson, eds. *Marketing Apocalypse*. London: Routledge, 1996.

Burrows, Peter, and Jim Kerstetter. "Profits: Still Going Strong." *Business Week* (May 1, 2000).

Byrnes, Nanette, and Ann Therese Palmer. "Toy Story—Can Toys 'R' Us CEO John Eyler Fix the Chain?" *Business Week* (December 4, 2000).

Carini, Maureen C. "Payless ShoeSource Stock Report." *Standard & Poor's* (February 23, 2002).

Churchill, Winston. *W.S. Marlborough: His Life and Times*. London: Harrap, 1947.

Cooke, James A. "From 3PL to 3PI." *Manufacturing.Net* (April 1, 2001).

Cortese, Amy. "Federal Express: Here Comes the Intranet." *Business Week* (February 26, 1996).

Crock, Stan. "The Pentagon Goes to B-School." *Business Week* (December 11, 1995).

Danzig, George, of Stanford University, interview with Damon Schechter (October 5, 2001).

Davis, Donald. *Why the North Won the Civil War*. Baton Rouge: University of Louisiana Press, 1960.

DeGeorge, Gail. "Ryder Sees the Logic of Logistics." *Business Week* (August 5, 1996).

Delaney, Robert V., and Rosalyn Wilson. "Managing Logistics in the Perfect Storm." *12th Annual State of Logistics Report*. Washington, DC: Cass/ProLogis, 2001.

Director, Operational Test & Evaluation. "Global Combat Support System—Air Force." *U.S. Air Force Annual Report* (1997).

Director for Strategic Plans & Policy, U.S. Joint Armed Services. *Joint Vision 2020* (June 2000).

Drayer, R. W., of Supply Chain Insights, interview with Damon Schechter (March 18, 2002).

Drexler, K. Eric. *Engines of Creation*. New York: Random House, 1986.

Drucker, Peter. "The Economy's Dark Continent." *Fortune* (April 1966).

Drucker, Peter. "Physical Distribution: The Frontier of Modern Management." In *Readings in Physical Distribution*, edited by Donald Bowersox et al. New York: Macmillan, 1969.

Elting, John R. *Swords around a Throne: Napoleon's Grande Army.* London: De Capo Press, 1988.

Engardio, Pete. "Why the Supply Chain Broke Down." *Business Week* (March 19, 2001).

Engels, Frederic. *Alexander the Great and the Logistics of the Macedonian Army.* Berkeley: University of California Press, 1978.

Ezell, Virginia, of U.S. Army Materiel Command, interview with Damon Schechter (December 3, 2001).

Faste, Rolf A. "Perceiving Needs." A paper for the *Society of Automotive Engineers* (1988).

Federal Express. *Annual Report*, 2000.

Foxton, P. D. *Powering War: Modern Land Force Logistics.* London: Brassey's, 1982.

Garamone, Jim. "Joint Vision 2020 Emphasizes Full-Spectrum Dominance." *American Forces Information Service* (June 2, 2000).

Goldbaugh, Dennis E., of the U.S. Military Academy, interview with Damon Schechter (November 27, 2001).

Goldberg, Stephanie B. "Supply-Chain Squeeze." *Business Week* (April 23, 2001).

Goldratt, Eliyahu. *The Goal.* Great Barrington, Mass.: North River Press, 1984.

Gurley, J. William "The Smartest Price War Ever." *CNET News* (June 25, 2001).

Guthrie, C. "The Importance of Wellington." *Daily Telegraph* (London) (October 7, 2001).

Halberstam, David. *The Reckoning.* New York: Morrow, 1986.

Hamilton, David P. "Chip Giant Places Huge Bet on Starting from Scratch." *Wall Street Journal* (June 4, 2001).

Hayward, P.H.C., ed. *Jane's Dictionary of Military Terms*. London: Alan Ross, 1975.

Heiser, Joseph M., Jr. *A Soldier Supporting Soldiers*. Washington, DC: Government Printing Office, 1996.

Helfert, Erich A. *Techniques of Financial Analysis: A Practical Guide to Managing and Measuring Business Performance*. New York: McGraw-Hill, 1996.

Henkoff, Ronald. "Delivering the Goods." *Fortune* (November, 1994).

Holmes, Richard, ed. *The Oxford Companion to Military History*. New York: Oxford University Press, 2001.

Hooper, Jack, of the Defense Logistics Agency, interview with Damon Schechter (November 28, 2001).

Hunter, Dick. "How Dell Keeps from Stumbling." *BusinessWeek* (May 14, 2001).

Ince, John F. "Supply Chain Management: Back to Basics." *Upside Magazine* (June 4, 2000).

Johnson, N. "JTAV Tells Military Where the 'Staff' Is." *Dimensions* (April/May 1998).

Jones, Archer. *The Art of War*. London: Harrap, 1988.

Keegan, John, interview with Gordon F. Sander and Damon Schechter (August 12, 2001).

Keegan, John. *The History of Warfare*. New York: Vintage, 1993.

Keegan, John. *The Mask of Command*. New York: Penguin USA, 1987.

Keenan, Faith. "Logistics Gets a Little Respect." *BusinessWeek* (November 20, 2000).

Kelley, Tom. *The Art of Innovation: Lessons in Creativity from IDEO, America's Leading Design Firm*. New York: Doubleday, 2001.

Kenny, J., of 3Com, interview with Damon Schechter (April 10, 2001).

Kobacker, Alfred, formerly of The Kobacker Company, interview with Damon Schechter (February 26, 2002).

Kobacker, John, formerly of The Kobacker Company, interview with Damon Schechter (February 18, 2002).

Kopczak, Laura Rock. "Apple Computer's Supplier Hubs: A Tale of Three Cities." *Stanford Global Supply Chain Management Forum* (1996).

Kotler, Philip. *Marketing Management: Analysis, Planning, Implementation and Control.* Upper Saddle River, N.J.: Prentice Hall, 1994.

Kransdorrf, A. "High Stock Levels—Not the Answer to Volatile Demand." *Financial Times* (June 4, 1982).

LaLonde, Bernard. "Evolution of the Integrated Logistics Concept. In *The Logistics Handbook*, edited by James Robeson et al. New York: Free Press, 1994.

LaLonde, Bernard, and Leslie Dawson. "Early Development of Physical Distribution Thought." In *Readings in Physical Distribution*, edited by Donald Bowersox et al. New York: Macmillan, 1969.

Larkin, John G., and Anthony P. Gallo. "Some Thoughts on Third Party Logistics." Working paper (November, 1996).

Larson, P. D., and B. Gammelgaard. "The Logistics Triad: Barriers and Facilitators." A paper for *The Nordic Logistics Research Network* (June 2001).

Lasiter, Timothy. *Balanced Sourcing: Cooperation and Competition in Supplier Relationships.* San Francisco: Jossey-Bass, 1988.

Lee, Hau L., and Seungjin Whang. "The Bullwhip Effect in Supply Chains." *Sloan Management Review* (Spring 1997).

Lewin, Ronald. *Slim: The Standard Bearer.* London: Wordsmith Editions, 1988.

Machiavelli, Nicolò. *The Prince*. New York: Buccaneer Books, 1994.

Macksey, Kenneth. *For Want of a Nail*. London: Brassey's, 1989.

Magnusson, Paul. "Q&A with Air Force Secretary James Roche." *Business Week* (February 11, 2002).

Magretta, Joan. "The Power of Virtual Integration: An Interview with Dell Computer's Michael Dell." *Harvard Business Review* (March/April 1998).

Master, James, and Terrance Pohlen. "Evolution of the Logistics Profession." *The Logistics Handbook*, edited by James Robeson et al. New York: Free Press, 1994.

McCarthy, E. J. *Basic Marketing*. Homewood, IL: Richard D. Irwin, 1975.

McFeely, William. *Grant*. New York: Norton, 1981.

McWilliams, Gary. "Dell Fine-Tunes Its PC Pricing to Gain an Edge in Slow Market." *Wall Street Journal* (June 8, 2001).

McWilliams, Gary, and Joseph B. White. "Others Want to Figure Out How to Adopt Dell Model." *Wall Street Journal* (December 1, 1999).

Miller, Michael J. "View from the Top." *PC Magazine* (September, 2001).

Morell, Andrea L. "The Forgotten Child of the Supply Chain." *Manufacturing.Net* (May 15, 2001).

O'Byron, Linda. "NBR's Memorial Day Special: How eCommerce Is Changing Business." *Nightly Business Report* (May 28, 2001).

Oliver, Keith, of Booz, Allen & Hamilton, London offices, interview with Gordon F. Sander (September 8, 2001).

Oliver, Keith, Anne Chung, and Nick Samanich. "Beyond Utopia: The Realist's Guide to Internet-Enabled Supply Chain Management." *Strategy + Business* (Issue Two, 2001).

O'Neill, William. *A Democracy at War*. Cambridge: Harvard University Press, 1993.

Pagonis, William G., of Sears, Roebuck, interview with Damon Schechter (September 20, 2001).

Pagonis, William G. *Moving Mountains: Lessons in Leadership and Logistics from the Gulf War*. Boston: Harvard Business School Press, 1992.

Payless ShoeSource. *Annual Report*, 1996–2000.

Peters, Katherine McIntire. "Joint Vision 2010 Still Focusing." *Government Executive Magazine* (February 1997).

Philips, Brad. "A Report on a California Design Company That Works to Create and Innovate. *Nightline*, ABC News (July 13, 1999).

Reese, Bud. "Physical Distribution: The Neglected Marketing Function. *Industrial Marketing* (October 1961).

Reese, Jennifer. "The Ups and Downs of Supply Chain Management." *Inbound Logistics* (December 1996).

Ristelhueber, Robert, and Jenniver Baljko Shah. "Supply Chain Chaos Blamed for Severity of Downturn." *EBN* (January 14, 2002).

Roche, James G., and Michael E. Ryan. "Joint Statement before the United States Senate Committee on Armed Services" (July 10, 2001).

Schwarzkopf, Norman. *Memoirs*. New York: Bantam, 1996.

Senge, Peter M. *The Fifth Discipline: The Art & Practice of the Learning Organization*. New York: Currency/Doubleday, 1990.

Shankland, Stephen. "Can McNealy Withstand the Heat?" *CNET News* (February 1, 2002).

Sharman, Graham. "The Rediscovery of Logistics." *Harvard Business Review* (September/October 1984).

Shaw, Arch. *An Approach to Business Problems*. Cambridge: Harvard University Press, 1916.

Sinclair, Joseph. *The Arteries of War: Military Transportation from Alexander the Great to the Falklands and Beyond*. Shrewsbury, England: Voyageur Press, 1992.

Skoll, Jeff, formerly of eBay, interview with Damon Schechter (November 29, 2001).

Slabodkin, G. "Maxwell AF Base Accepts First Part of Global Combat Support System." *DOD Computing* (October 1998).

Slim, William. *Defeat into Victory.* London: Cassell, 1956.

Stallkamp, Thomas T. "Should Suppliers Be Partners?" *Business-Week* (June 4, 2001).

Sterman, John D. "Flight Simulators for Management Education: The Beer Game." *Operations Research and Management Science Today* (October 1992).

Steven, John Simon. "The Art of Military Logistics." *Communications of the ACM New York* (June 2001).

Stewart, Thomas A. "Barely Managing: Beer Today, Gone Tomorrow." *Business 2.0* (August 2000).

Stock, James, and Douglas Lambert. *Strategic Logistics Management.* Homewood, IL: Richard D. Irwin, 1987.

Sun Microsystems. *Annual Report,* 2000.

Tamilia, Robert D., of the University of Quebec at Montreal, interview with Damon Schechter (March 18, 2002).

Tamilia, Robert D. "What Is the Importance of Logistics to Marketing Management." *Third International Meeting for Research in Logistics.* Trois-Riviéres: IMRL, 2000.

Taylor, W. L. "Joint Total Asset Visibility: Foundation of Focused Logistics." *Army Logistician* (May/June 2000).

Teitelbaum, Richard S. "What's Driving Return on Equity." *Fortune* (April 1996).

Trebilcock, Bob. "Careful! They May Be Watching!" *Manufacturing. Net* (May 15, 2001).

Van Creveld, Martin. *Supplying War: Logistics from Wallenstein to Patton.* Cambridge: Cambridge Press, 1977.

Varon, Elana, and John Stein Monroe. "Vendors Bullish on Cutting-Edge Procurements." *Federal Computer Week* (September 2, 1996).

Vogelstein, Fred. "Sun on the Ropes." *Fortune* (January 2002).

Wavell, Archibald. *Soldiers and Soldiering*. New York: Avery Publishing Group, 1986.

Wilson, Tim. "When Supply Chains Break: Event Tools Alert Partners." *Internet Week* (February 21, 2001).

Witzel, Morgen. *Marketing*. Bristol: Thoemmes, 2000.

Index